Teachings of the Warrior, Scholar and Sage

Book 3
Purpose, Philosophy, and the Path to Self-Mastery

By Jim Moltzan

Teachings of the Warrior, Scholar and Sage

Book 3
Purpose, Philosophy, and the Path to Self-Mastery

By Jim Moltzan

Disclaimer

This book is intended for informational and educational purposes only. It is not a substitute for professional medical, psychological, or mental health treatment. Nothing in this book should be interpreted as medical advice, mental health diagnosis, clinical intervention, or a guarantee of outcome. Readers experiencing significant emotional distress, trauma symptoms, or health concerns should consult a qualified healthcare or mental health professional.

The practices and concepts presented herein are offered as general guidance. The author does not promise or imply any specific results, nor is the author responsible for any adverse outcomes arising from the use or misuse of the information contained in this book. Use the material at your own discretion and risk.

The author has made every effort to ensure accuracy and completeness. However, the author makes no representations or warranties regarding the applicability, fitness, or completeness of the content for any individual reader.

ISBN: 978-1-958837-60-3

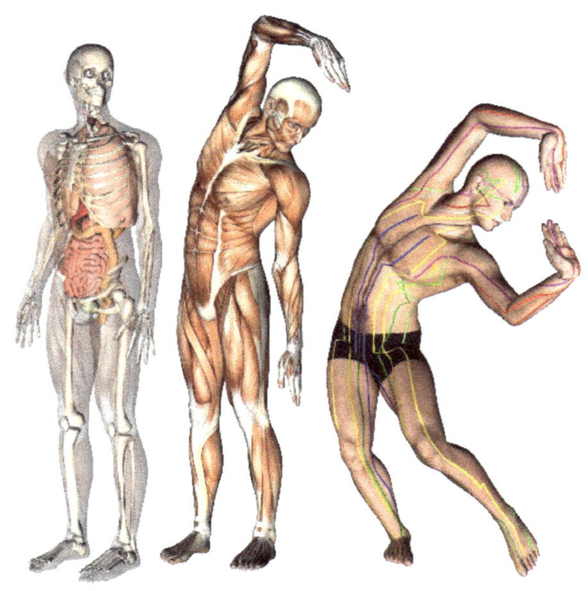

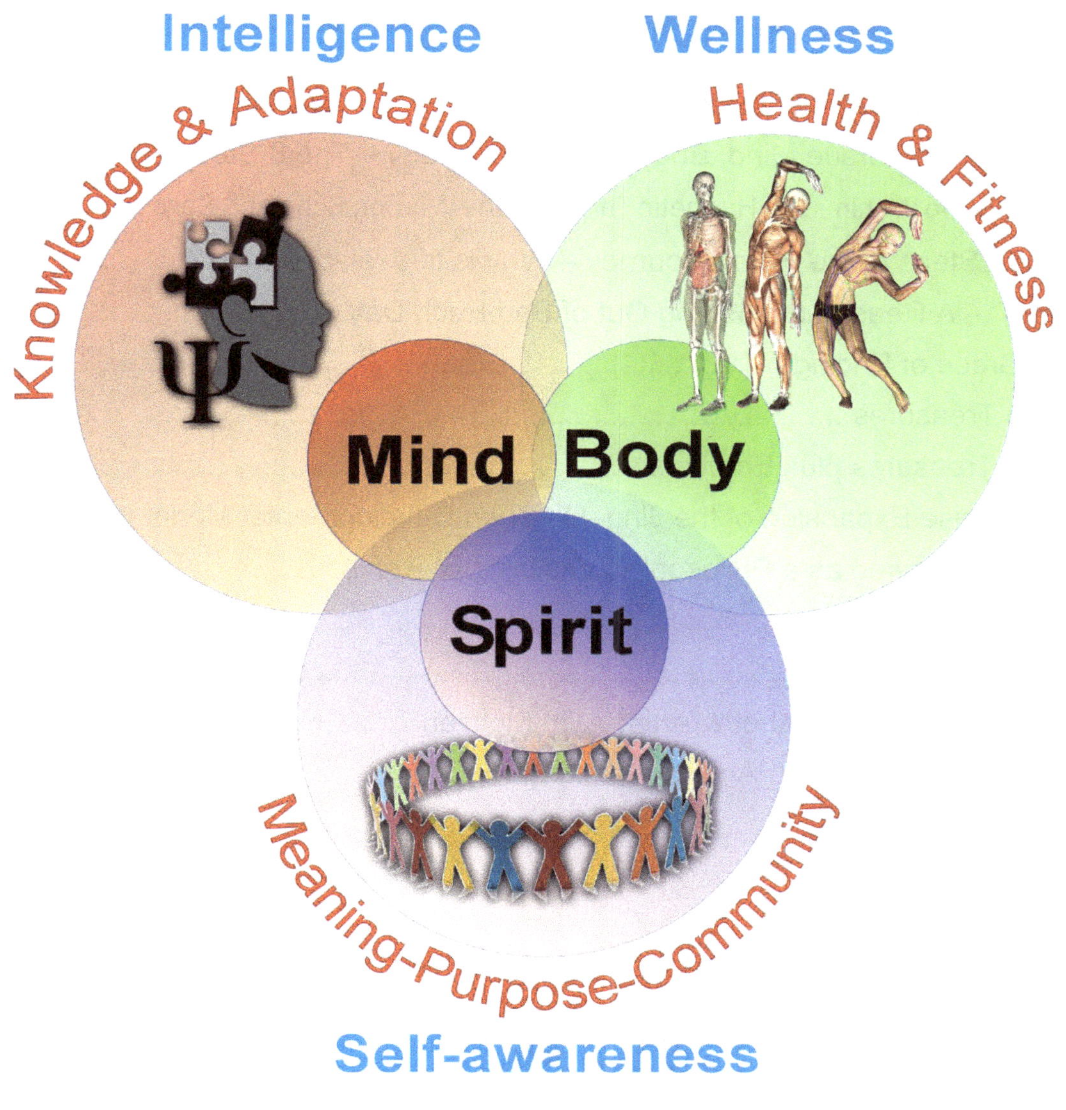

We become the architects of our lives once safety, awareness, and agency are restored.

Table of Contents

Preface

Wisdom from the Teachings of the Warrior, Scholar and Sage

This series was not written in a single sitting, nor conceived as a single book.
It is a collection of insights gathered over decades of practice, observation, teaching, and lived experience. Each essay within these volumes represents a moment of clarity, a realization shaped through time, discipline, and reflection. Some emerged through personal challenges, others through working with students, and many through quietly observing the patterns of human behavior as they repeat across generations.

Individually, these writings stand as short, focused reflections.

Together, they form a larger picture.

The intention behind this series is simple: to offer accessible entry points into ideas that are often overlooked, misunderstood, or buried beneath the noise of modern life. These are not abstract theories or rigid doctrines. They are practical observations about how people think, behave, adapt, struggle, and grow.

You will find themes of health, resilience, perception, identity, purpose, and personal responsibility woven throughout these pages. Some essays are grounded in the physical, exploring the body, breath, and the realities of aging. Others examine the mind, including how beliefs are formed, how reactions are conditioned, and how easily autonomy can be surrendered without awareness. Still others step back to consider broader philosophical questions regarding meaning, direction, and what it means to live well.

While the topics vary, the underlying thread remains consistent.

Human beings are capable of far more awareness, adaptability, and self-direction than they often realize.

The framework that ties these ideas together is expressed through the archetypes of the Warrior, the Scholar, and the Sage. These are not titles to be earned or identities to be claimed. They are aspects of development that exist within each individual.

The Warrior represents action, discipline, and the willingness to face reality directly.
The Scholar represents inquiry, understanding, and the pursuit of clarity.
The Sage represents integration, discernment, and the ability to apply knowledge with wisdom.

At different times in life, one may dominate over the others. The work is not to choose between them, but to cultivate all three.

These volumes are intentionally concise.

They are meant to be read in short segments, revisited over time, and reflected upon rather than consumed all at once. A single idea, properly understood and applied, carries more value than many ideas briefly encountered and forgotten.

You may find that certain essays resonate immediately, while others feel less relevant. This is natural. Meaning often emerges not from what is read, but from what is recognized at the right moment in one's life.

This series also serves another purpose.

It is a gateway.

The material presented here is drawn from a much larger body of work spanning decades and multiple volumes focused on holistic health, martial arts, philosophy, and human development. For those who find value in these pages, there is a deeper well of exploration available beyond this series.

However, nothing further is required.

If these essays prompt reflection, encourage action, or offer a shift in perspective, then they have already served their purpose.

There are no promises of transformation within these pages. Only the opportunity.

The responsibility for what is done with that opportunity remains where it always has been.

With the reader.

Author's Note:

On the Nature of These Writings

The writings contained within this series were not originally intended to be grouped together in this way.

They were developed over time, often as individual essays, reflections, or responses to questions that arose through teaching, conversation, and observation. Some were written to clarify a concept for students. Others emerged from personal experience, moments of insight, or the need to better understand patterns I was seeing repeatedly in both myself and others.

What you are reading here is not a single narrative, but a collection of distilled ideas.

Over the years, I have come to recognize that many of the same challenges continue to surface across different people, backgrounds, and stages of life. Issues related to health, stress, identity, purpose, and personal direction are not new, but they do seem to be increasingly intensified within the pace and structure of modern culture.

Rather than attempting to address everything within one continuous work, I have found value in isolating individual ideas and exploring them with clarity and focus. This allows each topic to stand on its own, while still contributing to a larger understanding of the human experience.

These essays reflect that approach.

My background spans more than four decades of study and practice in martial arts, breath training, and holistic health, combined with later academic work in psychology and human behavior. Over time, what began as a primarily physical discipline evolved into a broader inquiry into how the body, mind, and internal processes are interconnected.

I have worked with a wide range of individuals, from those seeking physical improvement, to those navigating stress, aging, or major life transitions. Across all of these experiences, certain patterns remain consistent.

How a person breathes affects how they move.
How they move affects how they feel.
How they feel affects how they think and respond.

These relationships are not theoretical. They are observable and, more importantly, they are trainable.

The language used throughout this series reflects a blend of influences. Traditional Chinese Medicine, Taoist philosophy, and internal martial arts provide one framework.

Modern psychology, physiology, and behavioral science provide another. While these systems often use different terminology, they frequently describe the same underlying processes.

My intention is not to promote one system over another, but to present ideas in a way that is practical, understandable, and applicable to everyday life.

It is also important to be clear about what this series is not.

It is not a step-by-step program.
It is not a fixed philosophy.
It is not a promise of transformation.

These writings are offered as points of reflection.

Some may resonate immediately. Others may not. In many cases, understanding develops over time, as experience provides context for the ideas being presented.

This series represents only a small portion of a much larger body of work. Many of these concepts are explored in greater depth across my other books, where topics are expanded, structured, and developed more fully.

Here, the focus is different.

These are concise, accessible entries into broader themes, designed to be read, considered, and revisited as needed.

If they encourage you to think more clearly, observe more carefully, or take more responsibility for your own development, then they have fulfilled their purpose.

Beyond that, the work is yours.

- *Jim Moltzan*

1. An Introduction to the philosophy of the Warrior, Scholar, and Sage

Within this framework there are 3 distinct mindsets or phases, when it comes to training and self-improvement. However, this concept can also be applied towards various other walks of life from the soldier, the martial artist, the yoga practitioner, the car mechanic, the nurse, the carpenter, the parent, among many other walks of life, and all ages, races, and orientations.

• **The Warrior** - focuses mostly on the physical, the body, the movement, doing the work, getting the job done, defending, protecting and in general, looking out for others. In modern society, we can find warriors in various professions that require physical and mental strength, resilience, and a proactive approach to challenges. Examples include soldiers who protect their countries, Law enforcement and firefighters who risk their lives to save others, athletes who train rigorously to excel in their sports, parents and people who advocate for the benefit of others.

• **The Scholar** - focuses on the history, the backstory, the mechanics, understanding how, when, where and why things work. Scholars are those who delve into knowledge, research, and the understanding of their fields. Modern examples include scientists who explore the mysteries of the universe, historians who study and interpret past events, educators who impart knowledge and foster intellectual growth in their students, leaders in the workplace who teach their employees their craft and those who are looking for answers to other issues.

• **The Sage** - draws upon life experiences from being a warrior or scholar to make wise decisions. Examples in modern society include therapists who help individuals navigate their mental health journeys, mentors who provide guidance to their protégés, community leaders who use their understanding of societal dynamics to create positive change, and parents or individuals that mentor others. This list is by no means, exclusive.

This progression reflects the Confucian path of xiushen or self-cultivation, which begins with the somatic re-calibration of the body, proceeds to the iterative cultivation of the mind, and culminates in the transmutation of higher virtue and self-awareness. A sequence mirrored in the stages of what some martial artists refer to as "Mudo training."

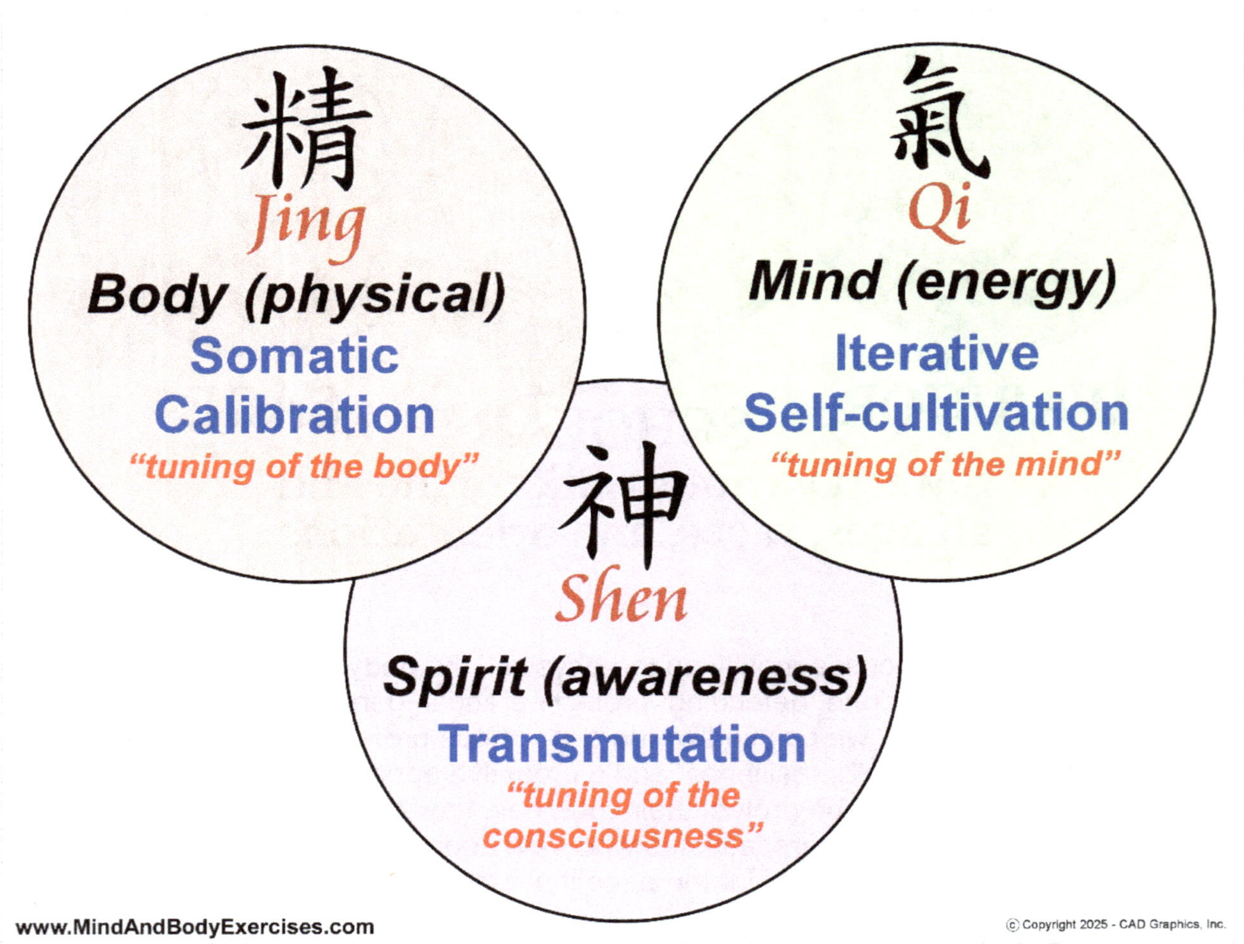

There is much relevance in this archetypal triad today. In the modern world, the martial path is often misunderstood as archaic or irrelevant, reduced to competitive sport, mere self-defense techniques or an afternoon activity for young children. Yet the deeper essence of Mudo, and its embodiment in the Warrior-Scholar-Sage archetype, remains profoundly relevant. Modern life presents its own battlefields: stress, distraction, ethical dilemmas, and existential uncertainty. Physical strength remains essential, but also critical thinking, emotional intelligence, self-awareness and spiritual depth. Who truly does not desire to have a stronger body, a sharp mind and a connection to something greater than the self?

Contemporary martial artists and holistic practitioners increasingly recognize the necessity of integrating these three dimensions. The physical discipline of martial training enhances health, vitality, and resilience; the intellectual discipline of study sharpens judgment and fosters adaptability; and the spiritual discipline of ethical reflection and self-awareness nurtures compassion and purpose. Together, these qualities form a foundation for leadership, community service, and meaningful living.

Moreover, this archetype of the Warrior, Scholar and Sage, provides a powerful framework for self-transformation. It teaches that true strength is not brute force, but disciplined action guided by wisdom; that knowledge is hollow without moral grounding; and that virtue, separated from courage and clarity, cannot manifest in the world. The individual who cultivates all three dimensions approaches the classical idea of the junzi,or the “complete human” who embodies harmony between Heaven, Earth, and humanity.

Psychologist Carl Jung referred to this as Coniunctio, describing the concept for the psychological "union of opposites" — such as conscious/unconscious or anima/animus. Similarily, psychologist Abraham Maslow's self-actualization is the pinnacle of his hierarchy of needs, representing the innate human drive to fulfill one's unique potential, become the best version of oneself, and find meaning, creativity, and personal growth. A Single Path, can have Many Expressions: The apparent distinction between Mudo and the Way of the Warrior, Scholar, and Sage dissolves under closer examination.

They are, in essence, two ways of describing the same holistic process of the cultivation of the body, the mind, and the spirit in pursuit of human excellence. Taoism refers to this simply as living in harmony with, the Way. Mudo is the vehicle; the Warrior, Scholar, and Sage are the milestones and manifestations along the journey.

This integrated vision has guided martial practitioners, philosophers, and sages across centuries and cultures. It remains as vital today as it was in the age of the samurai or the scholar-warrior bureaucrat. For in every era, the human being who embodies courage, wisdom, and virtue, with the warrior who can fight when necessary, the scholar who seeks truth, and the sage who acts from compassion, stand as a living expression of the Way itself.

It is usually not too difficult to see the warriors, scholars and sages all around us in our everyday lives and travels. For those seeking to cultivate self-mastery, they just need to look in the mirror to find them, in each and every one of us. Many of my later books from numbers 31-39 delve deeper into this theme of the warrior, scholar and Sage in everyday life.

2. A Method to Pursue Mind, Body & Spirit Harmony – The 8-Step Path

Quite often I hear people talking about wanting to pursue a better understanding of the mind, body and spiritual (or self-awareness) relationship. Usually, most people have little understanding of this concept beyond repeating someone else's words. Understanding of this relationship cannot come from someone else but rather grown or cultivated in oneself from personal knowledge, experience and wisdom. There are no books, shortcuts, seminars, gurus or masters that can do this for the individual; however, they may help guide one to reach self-realization. I am sharing here what I have learned and have tried to live as part of my daily life. Spirituality and religion are often lumped together but have rather distinctly different meanings. With this video, I look at spirituality more as a level of self-awareness, purpose and life direction and not necessarily a membership to any particular religion or belief system.

A long-understood method of achieving harmony between one's mind, body and spirit, is this 8-Step Path. It has its origin in the ancient Chinese philosophy of Daoism but is highly relative to modern culture. This is by no means the only method to find this harmony of mind, body and spirit. It is a time-proven method that I have learned and have tried to cultivate for many years.

The figure "8" is important to understand that as the infinity circle, there is no beginning nor end to entering into this process. It is a journey of self-awareness that can be entered into at any point throughout one's lifetime. Life is a challenge, and so is staying on this path of self-improvement. The reward is at the end of one's journey, knowing that they have pursued a meaningful life with direction and purpose.

This graphic shows how the 8 steps are all interconnected.

The 8-step Path is rooted in **Eight Keys of Wisdom, which in turn** are rooted in **Taoist, Confucian, and Buddhist principles**, such as: **Wu Wei (or Effortless Action)** in Taoism, similar to "Be Like Bamboo" reflecting flexibility and balance. Also, **Right Conduct and Ethics** found in Confucianism, and similar to "The True-Right-Correct Method." And lastly, **Mindfulness and Detachment from Thought found** in Buddhism and reflected in "Stop Being Drunk on Your Own Thoughts."

The **Eight Keys of Wisdom** serve as guiding principles for integrating mindfulness and meditation into daily life. Here's a deeper look at each:

1. Reflection (Know Your True Self)

• This key emphasizes self-awareness and authenticity.

• It encourages recognizing personal strengths, weaknesses, and emotional patterns.

• Understanding oneself allows for conscious decision-making and alignment with one's true nature.

The 8-Step Path to Achieve the Best Version of You

www.MindAndBodyExercises.com

A long-understood method of achieving harmony between one's mind, body and spirit, is this 8-Step Path. It has its origin in the ancient Chinese philosophy of Daoism but is highly relative to modern culture. The figure "8" is important to understand that as the infinity circle, there is no beginning nor end to entering into this process. It is a journey of self-awareness that can be entered into at any point throughout one's lifetime. Life is a challenge, and so is staying on this path of self-improvement. The reward is at the end of one's journey, knowing that they have pursued a meaningful life with direction and purpose.

1 Learning to Know Your "True Self"

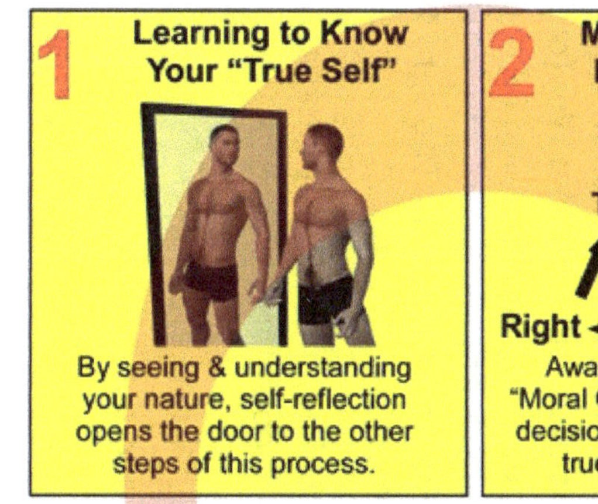

By seeing & understanding your nature, self-reflection opens the door to the other steps of this process.

2 Making Correct Daily Choices

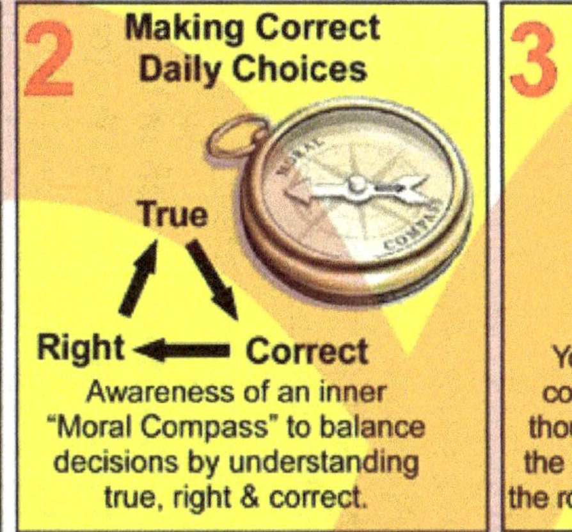

Awareness of an inner "Moral Compass" to balance decisions by understanding true, right & correct.

3 Overcome Delusion of Your Thoughts & Ideas

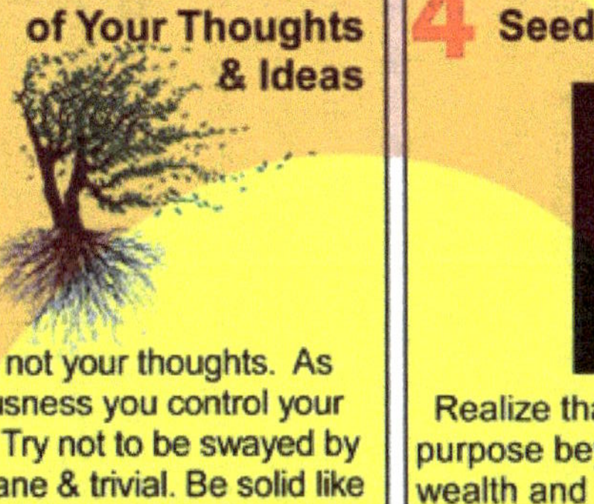

You are not your thoughts. As consciousness you control your thoughts. Try not to be swayed by the mundane & trivial. Be solid like the root & not flippant like the leaves.

4 Cultivate Good Seeds to Pass On

Realize that you have a higher purpose beyond gaining material wealth and status. Be the light at the end of the tunnel.

5 Attain Honor

Live by principle - stand firm in what you believe, while allowing challenges to flow around you. Stand like a mountain, flow like a river.

6 Change Your Reality

Understand that you are in control of your life and the choices you make determine your success or failure within your reality.

7 Become a Living Vessel of Wisdom

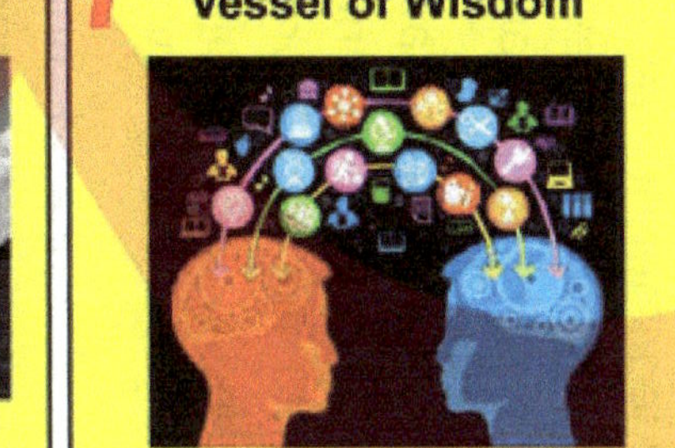

Knowledge alone is not power. The sharing of our knowledge, is when knowledge becomes powerful.

8 Draw on Nature's Power

Cultivate a strong mind, body & spirit by connecting to nature's fire, water & wind with sitting, standing & moving exercises.

2. Make Correct Choices (The True-Right-Correct Method)

• Rooted in Eastern philosophy, this principle teaches the importance of seeking truth and making ethical choices.

• "True" represents inner wisdom, "Right" signifies ethical action, and "Correct" ensures that actions align with both personal integrity and universal balance.

3. Overcome Delusion (Stop Being Drunk on Your Own Thoughts)

• Encourages detachment from overthinking and emotional reactivity.

• Teaches mindfulness techniques to observe thoughts without being consumed by them.

• Helps develop clarity and inner calm by breaking free from habitual negative thinking.

4. How Will You Be Remembered? (Plant Good Seeds)

• Invites reflection on one's legacy and the impact of actions on others.

• Encourages living with purpose, kindness, and awareness of how one's presence affects the world.

• Turn on your light, becoming an inspiration and not a warning to others

5. Seek Connectedness & Honor (Be Like a Mountain)

• Focuses on building meaningful relationships through respect, integrity, and compassion.

• Recognizes the interconnectedness of all people and the importance of honoring those connections.

• Teaches that true strength comes from unity rather than isolation.

6. Change Your Reality for the Better

• Encourages personal responsibility in shaping one's experiences.

• Highlights the power of perspective—choosing optimism and proactive behavior over victimhood.

• Teaches how shifting internal attitudes can influence external circumstances.

7. Become a Vessel of Wisdom (It Only Takes One Match to Light a Thousand)

• Demonstrates the power of small actions in creating widespread change.

• Encourages leading by example, where one positive act can inspire many others.

• Stresses that transformation begins with individual effort, no matter how small.

8. Draw from Nature's Energies (Be Like Bamboo)

• Symbolizes resilience, flexibility, and strength.

• Encourages adaptability in the face of challenges while maintaining inner strength.

• Teaches that true power lies in balance, being strong yet flexible, firm yet yielding.

As I commented upon earlier, this is by no means the only method to find and cultivate harmony of mind, body and spirit. It is a time-proven method that I have learned and have tried to cultivate for many years.

3. As Above, So Within - The Hermetic Thread of the Warrior, Scholar & Sage

Every comprehensive system of human transformation contains a bridge, one that links the physical body to the invisible dimensions of mind and spirit. In the Eastern traditions this bridge is expressed through ***Jing*** (essence), ***Qi*** (vital energy), ***and Shen*** (consciousness). In the developmental framework I teach, it appears as the **Warrior, Scholar, and Sage**. In the Western esoteric lineage, the same bridge is known as **Hermeticism**, a philosophical and spiritual system attributed to Hermes Trismegistus, the "Thrice-Great" master of physical, intellectual, and spiritual wisdom.

These are not parallel systems by coincidence. They are structurally identical expressions of the same universal process of human refinement, or the ascent from embodiment to insight, and from insight to integrated wisdom. Across cultures and centuries, the language changes, but the architecture remains.

Hermeticism arises from Hellenistic Egypt, a fusion of Greek philosophy, Egyptian spirituality, early science, medicine, astronomy, and metaphysics (Copenhaver, 1992; Fowden, 1993). Its core message is simple but profound: **reality is mental, patterned, cyclical, lawful, and capable of conscious transformation**. The most famous Hermetic maxim from the *Emerald Tablet* expresses this truth succinctly:

"As above, so below; as within, so without."

This is not merely poetic symbolism. It is a functional statement of psychospiritual law: what is refined in the body shapes the mind; what is clarified in the mind refines the spirit; what is awakened in the spirit returns to illuminate the body.

The Eight Hermetic Principles and Their Living Expression

Hermetic philosophy is traditionally organized into eight fundamental principles (seven classical principles plus the unifying axiom of Integration & Moral Alignment). These principles are not abstract metaphysics; they describe how transformation actually happens in daily life.

Below is a brief, applied summary of each.

1. Mentalism – "All is Mind."

Reality originates in consciousness.

Example:
Thought hygiene, attention control, emotional regulation, and metacognition all reflect the fact that perception shapes experience. In practice, this is where the **Scholar** refines Qi through disciplined awareness.

7 HERMETIC PRINCIPLES

1. THE PRINCIPLE OF MENTALISM
ALL IS MIND, THE UNIVERSE IS MENTAL

2. THE PRINCIPLE OF CORRESPONDENCE
AS WITHIN, SO WITHOUT

3. THE PRINCIPLE OF VIBRATION
NOTHING RESTS, EVERYTHING MOVES, EVERYTHING VIBRATES

4. THE PRINCIPLE OF POLARITY
EVERYTHING HAS ITS OPPOSITE, IDENTICAL IN NATURE

5. THE PRINCIPLE OF RHYTHM
ALL THINGS RISE AND FALL

6. THE PRINCIPLE OF CAUSE AND EFFECT
CHANCE IS NOT BUT A NAME

7. THE PRINCIPLE OF GENDER
EVERYTHING CONTAINS MASCULINE AND FEMININE PRINCIPLES

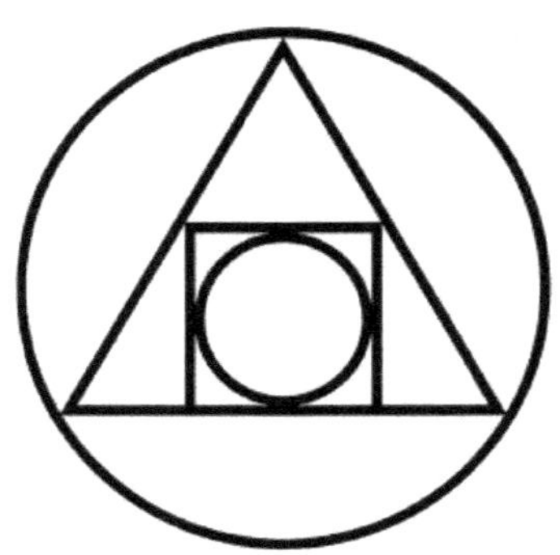

2. Correspondence – "As above, so below; as within, so without."

Patterns repeat across all levels of existence.

Example:
Organ–emotion relationships, archetypal symbolism, and synchronicity reflect this principle. The **Sage** expresses it through Shen-based integration and purpose.

3. Vibration – "Nothing rests; everything moves."

All things exist in motion and frequency.

Example:
Breath rhythm, posture, nervous system tone, and muscular tension all shape consciousness. This is the foundational work of the **Warrior**, refining Jing through somatic calibration.

4. Polarity – "Opposites are identical in nature, differing only in degree."

All dualities exist on a spectrum.

Example:
Fear and courage, stress and resilience, pain and growth are not opposites but transformations of the same continuum. This principle governs emotional alchemy and shadow integration.

5. Rhythm – "Everything flows in and out."

Nature moves in cycles.

Example:
Circadian rhythms, seasonal cycles, recovery cycles in training, and emotional tides all operate under rhythmic law. Ignoring rhythm leads to burnout; honoring it leads to longevity.

6. Cause and Effect – "Every cause has its effect."

Nothing is random.

Example:
Consistent practice compounds. Discipline produces capacity. Neglect produces decay. This principle governs training progression, psychological habit formation, and destiny itself.

7. Gender – "Masculine and feminine principles exist in everything."

All creation arises from active and receptive forces.

Example:
Stillness and motion, force and yielding, analysis and intuition are necessary partners. In internal alchemy this corresponds to ***Kan*** and ***Li***, or the inner marriage of fire and water.

8. The Unifying Principle – Integration & Moral Alignment

(Implicit throughout the Hermetic texts)

This is the **alchemical ascent** itself:
Matter → Energy → Consciousness → Unity
Warrior → Scholar → Sage
Jing → Qi → Shen

It describes the return of the fragmented human being to wholeness.

Hermeticism and Eastern Internal Alchemy: One Process, Two Languages

Western Hermeticism and Daoist **Neidan** (internal alchemy) describe the same three-stage refinement:

1. **Refining Jing (Warrior)** – stability, grounding, structure, breath, stance
2. **Refining Qi (Scholar)** – insight, emotional regulation, meaning
3. **Refining Shen (Sage)** – awareness, wisdom, unity, purpose

In Hermetic terms this mirror:

- Earth → Air → Fire → Ether
- Body → Mind → Spirit → Divine Mind
- Alchemy → Knowledge → Illumination → Union

The training of the body becomes the furnace of consciousness. The mind becomes the instrument of refinement. The spirit becomes the field of meaning.

Jung and Psychology as Modern Hermetic Science

Carl Jung recognized Western and Eastern alchemy as symbolic maps of **individuation**, or the integration of the unconscious and conscious psyche (Jung, 1968). He interpreted alchemical stages as:

- Shadow purification
- Integration of opposites
- Inner marriage (coniunctio)
- Emergence of the unified Self

This is precisely the **Warrior–Scholar–Sage** progression expressed in psychological language.

Why Hermeticism Matters Now

Modern culture suffers from a dangerous fragmentation:

- The **Warrior** has been reduced to stress and survival
- The **Scholar** to data without wisdom
- The **Sage** to abstraction without embodiment

Hermeticism restores their unity as a single ascending current of human evolution. It re-establishes the coherence between:

- Body and breath
- Thought and emotion
- Discipline and compassion
- Knowledge and service
- Identity and purpose

This blog summary introduces the deeper work now fully developed in my newest release:

Book 38 – *Hermeticism: Its Relevance to the Teachings of the Warrior, Scholar & Sage*

This volume stands at the architectural center of my entire body of work. It reveals:

- How the Warrior becomes the Scholar
- How the Scholar becomes the Sage
- How the Sage returns to unity
- And how all three operate simultaneously as a single living process

It is not a theoretical book. It is a map of transformation, as it seeks to integrate Hermetic law, Eastern internal alchemy, Jungian psychology, nervous system science, breathwork, ethics, and the meaning-making process of human life.

Hermeticism is not something to believe. It is something to practice, embody, and become.

As above, so within.
As within, so becomes the world.

References:

Copenhaver, B. P. (1992). *Hermetica: The Greek Corpus Hermeticum and the Latin Asclepius*. Cambridge University Press.

Faivre, A. (1994). *Access to Western Esotericism*. SUNY Press.

Fowden, G. (1993). The Egyptian Hermes: A historical approach to the late pagan mind. Princeton University Press. https://archive.org/details/egyptianhermeshi0000fowd

Jung, C. G. (1968). Alchemical studies (R. F. C. Hull, Trans.). Princeton University Press. https://www.jungiananalysts.org.uk/wp-content/uploads/2018/07/C.-G.-Jung-Collected-Works-Volume-13_-Alchemical-Studies.pdf

Mahé, J.-P. (1998). The treatise on the "Emerald Tablet." *Journal of the Warburg and Courtauld Institutes, 61*, 1–20.

Principe, L. M. (2013). *The Secrets of Alchemy*. University of Chicago Press.

The Philosopher's Stone

4. The 12 Steps of the Hero's Journey – Why is this relative to us?

The concept of the "Hero's Journey" comes from Joseph Campbell who was a writer, mythologist, and lecturer. Campbell introduced this idea in his book "The Hero with a Thousand Faces," which was published in 1949. The theme underlying in the Hero's Journey is that many myths, stories and legends, from differing cultures throughout the world and throughout history follow a similar pattern or structure. Psychologist Carl Jung referred to this innate relationship as the collective unconscious. The Hero's Journey consists of roughly 12 distinct stages for a "chosen one" to navigate. Specific details may vary from culture to culture, but the overall structure remains fairly consistent. Examples would be that of Gilgamesh (Sumerian/Babylonian Mythology), King Arthur (Arthurian Legends), The Odyssey and Jason and the Argonauts (Greek Mythology), The Ramayana (Hindu Mythology), Sun Wukong (Journey to the West – Chinese Mythology), Inanna's Descent to the Underworld (Sumerian Mythology), and Siegfried, the dragon slayer (Germanic mythology).

The Hero's Journey and The 12 Phases

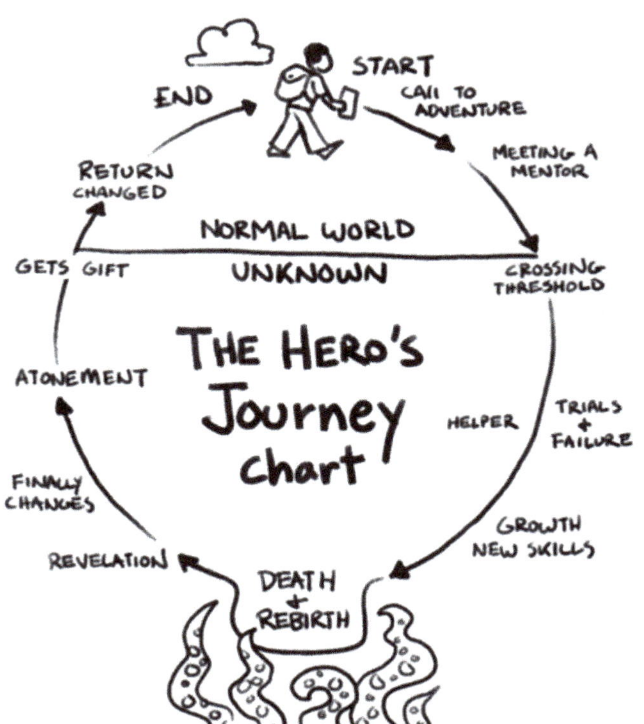

1st Act (The Known)

1. The Ordinary World
2. Call to Adventure
3. Refusal of The Call
4. Meeting The Mentor
5. Crossing The Threshold

2nd Act (The Adventure)

6. Tests, Allies, Enemies
7. Approaching The Inner Cave
8. The Ordeal
9. Seize The Reward

3rd Act (Chance to Make It Right)

10. The Road Back Home
11. Resurrection, Atonement
12. Return with The Elixir

This structure of storytelling has also been popularized by modern authors of books and movies such as Lord of the Rings, Harry Potter, The Hunger Games and maybe most widely known of "Star Wars". George Lucas of Star Wars was inspired by Campbell's writings, but the two did not meet until well after Lucas had already produced his famous movies. I think that if we look carefully and reflect inward, we may be able to also see the pattern of the hero's journey in each of our own lives. Why is this important? Because seeing our lives from this perspective can help to add clarity and focus to the unique meaning and purpose that we all possess but are not always aware of.

I find Sam Keen and Anne Valley Fox's Your Mythic Journey published in 1973, to be quite relevant to current cultural and societal issues. Specifically, that of myths being defined as lies or something opposite of being factual. I too used to think of myths as lies or mere stories to entertain us, until I became educated otherwise to this stigma. Keen elaborates that myths are a strict set of interconnected stories, customs, rituals, and rites, that serve to inform us while providing a sense of meaning, purpose, and direction to an individual, a family, a community, or culture. Keen expresses that telling of myths, ancient as well as modern have fallen to the wayside due to advances in technologies and the evolution of cultures and societies. When particular things can be seen as "good," there is always the other opposite or contrasting perspective of there existing some amount of "bad." While technology might be a factor in people choosing to not write their stories down as much as in years ago or choose to commit them to memory, because they know that they can always just look them up on the internet. The other side of this coin is that modern technology has opened up the ability for more people to access other nations' information bases and various cultures' stories, myths, and knowledge, literally from the comfort and convenience of their own homes. In years past if someone cared to pursue learning about a particular culture, they might very well be best informed if they were to travel across the oceans to find a source that they was willing to share. Today we just pick up our smartphone to travel in our thoughts to the other side of the world.

I have been immersed in a Taoist lifestyle for over 40 years, both from my martial arts and Traditional Chinese Medicine (TCM) background and study of this philosophy. With this in mind, I am drawn to see the yin and yang or the balance and contrast, in all things. This concept of yin and yang dates back thousands of years where Taoism has its origins around 500 BCE. Perhaps Taoism came about from the passing of myths to one another, or some myths may have come about from those having studied Taoism. Or maybe both are true, a debate for another discussion. Keen's words have yin and yang written deep throughout them, as he hints that the contrast between heroes and enemies, is what gives meaning to either side.

Keen later goes on to speak of the inner voices of our ancestors and those around us, that often run through our minds. I have come to know this as our inner dialogue, and when not in check, referred to as the "monkey mind" that is constantly and incessantly jumping from one thought or story to another. Organizing our stories and our myths in our own mind is the challenge. These stories can offer us purpose and meaning to each of us in our own individual and unique ways in spite of standing on the shoulders of those who came before us with their stories and myths. Current popular culture in the US seems somewhat focused upon people needing to come to some realization of "their truth" as opposed to what Keen speaks of as "their story." Can various different people having the same experience have different truths? I think not, but they can definitely have different stories of their own unique experience. An underlying theme that Keen speaks of is the need for someone to stand in the shoes of another, if they are to truly understand another's story, whether in their myths, culture, traditions, symbols, etc.

I find Keen's comments about how few people really know the depth of their own thoughts and imaginations quite accurate. I see more people concerned with what is going on within the virtual computer-generated and online social worlds outside of themselves, rather than understanding what is happening within their own minds. Some people can claim to know about driving a race car in virtual reality when they actually only know how to drive a standard vehicle in the physical world. Learning to understand and differentiate our public and private selves or "discovering our many selves" as Keen states, is a bit of foreshadowing of what I read later as some strong Carl Jung influences of personas, and archetypes as well as Sigmund Freud's concepts of the id and ego.

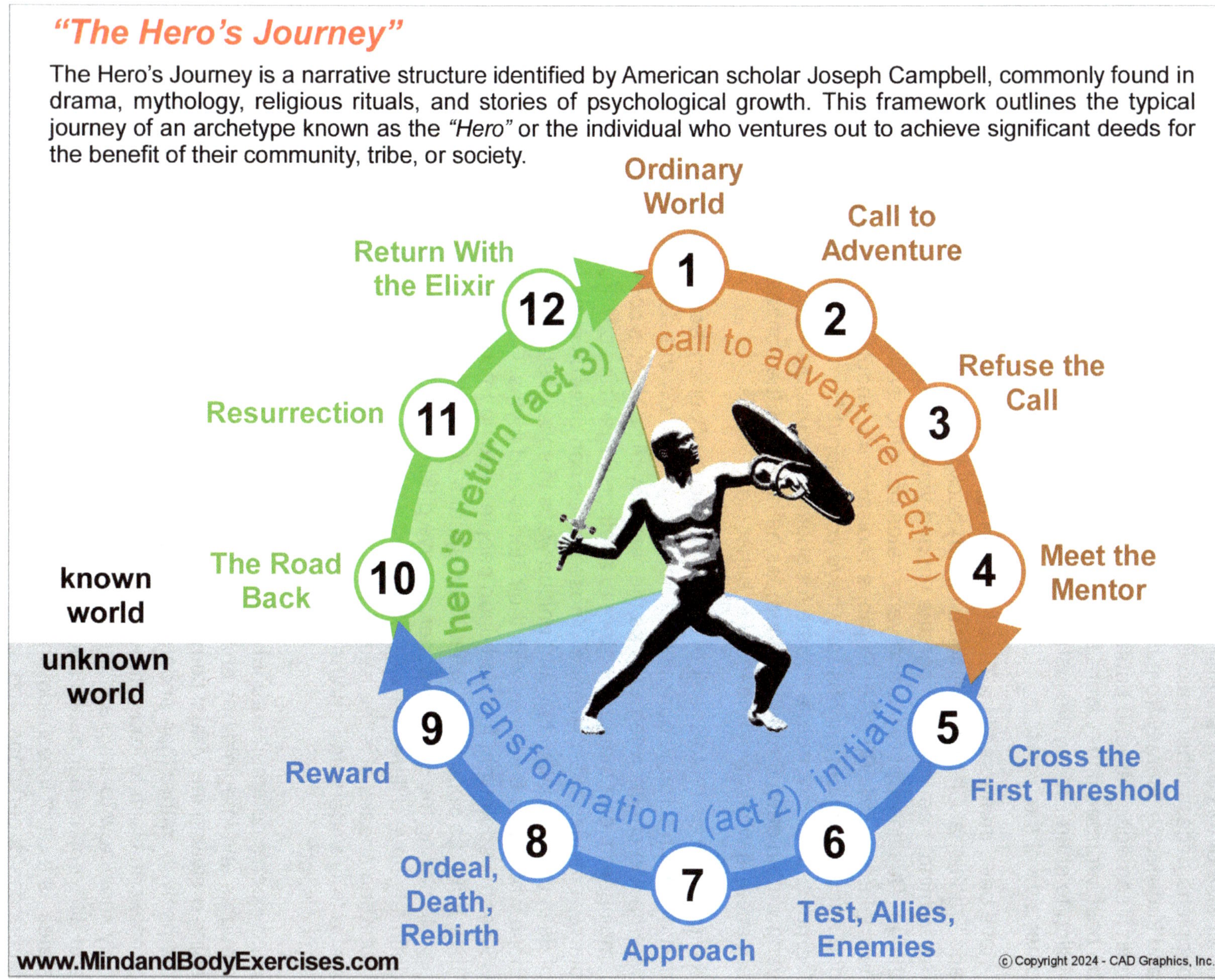
"The Hero's Journey"
The Hero's Journey is a narrative structure identified by American scholar Joseph Campbell, commonly found in drama, mythology, religious rituals, and stories of psychological growth. This framework outlines the typical journey of an archetype known as the *"Hero"* or the individual who ventures out to achieve significant deeds for the benefit of their community, tribe, or society.
known world
unknown world
1 Ordinary World
2 Call to Adventure
3 Refuse the Call
4 Meet the Mentor
5 Cross the First Threshold
6 Test, Allies, Enemies
7 Approach
8 Ordeal, Death, Rebirth
9 Reward
10 The Road Back
11 Resurrection
12 Return With the Elixir
call to adventure (act 1)
initiation
transformation (act 2)
hero's return (act 3)
www.MindandBodyExercises.com
© Copyright 2024 - CAD Graphics, Inc.

The 12 steps of the hero's journey:

1. **The Ordinary World**

The hero, uneasy, uncomfortable or unaware, is introduced sympathetically so the audience can identify with the situation or dilemma. The hero is shown against a background of environment, heredity, and personal history. Some kind of polarity in the hero's life is pulling in different directions and causing stress.

2. **The call to adventure**

Something shakes up the situation, either from external pressures or from something rising up from deep within, so the hero must face the beginnings of change.

3. **Refusal of the call**

The hero feels the fear of the unknown and tries to turn away from the adventure, however briefly. Alternately, another character may express the uncertainty and danger ahead.

4. **Meeting with the mentor**

The hero comes across a seasoned traveler of the world who gives him or her training, equipment, or advice that will help on the journey. Or the hero reaches within to a source of courage and wisdom.

5. **Crossing the threshold**

At the end of Act One, the hero commits to leaving the Ordinary World and entering a new region or condition with unfamiliar rules and values.

6. **Tests, allies, and enemies**

The hero is tested and sorts out allegiances in the Special World.

7. **Approach**

The hero and newfound allies prepare for the major challenge in the Special world.

8. **The ordeal**

Near the middle of the story, the hero enters a central space in the Special World and confronts death or faces his or her greatest fear. Out of the moment of death comes a new life.

9. **The reward**

The hero takes possession of the treasure won by facing death. There may be celebration, but there is also danger of losing the treasure again.

10. **The road back**

About three-fourths of the way through the story, the hero is driven to complete the adventure, leaving the Special World to be sure the treasure is brought home. Often a chase scene signals the urgency and danger of the mission.

11. **The resurrection**

At the climax, the hero is severely tested once more on the threshold of home. He or she is purified by a last sacrifice, another moment of death and rebirth, but on a higher and more complete level. By the hero's action, the polarities that were in conflict at the beginning are finally resolved.

12. **Return with the elixir**

The hero returns home or continues the journey, bearing some element of the treasure that has the power to transform the world as the hero has been transformed.

I feel that we are all pursuing a hero's journey on some level as we all manage and cope with our daily trials and tribulations. However, it is up to the individual to reach some inner clarity and cultivation of character to better understand how this concept applies to their story.

References:

Campbell, J. (1949). The hero with a thousand faces. Pantheon Books.

Keen, S. (1989). Your Mythic Journey: Finding Meaning in Your Life Through Writing and Storytelling. TarcherPerigee

5. "Ikigai" – A Reason for Getting Out of Bed Each Day

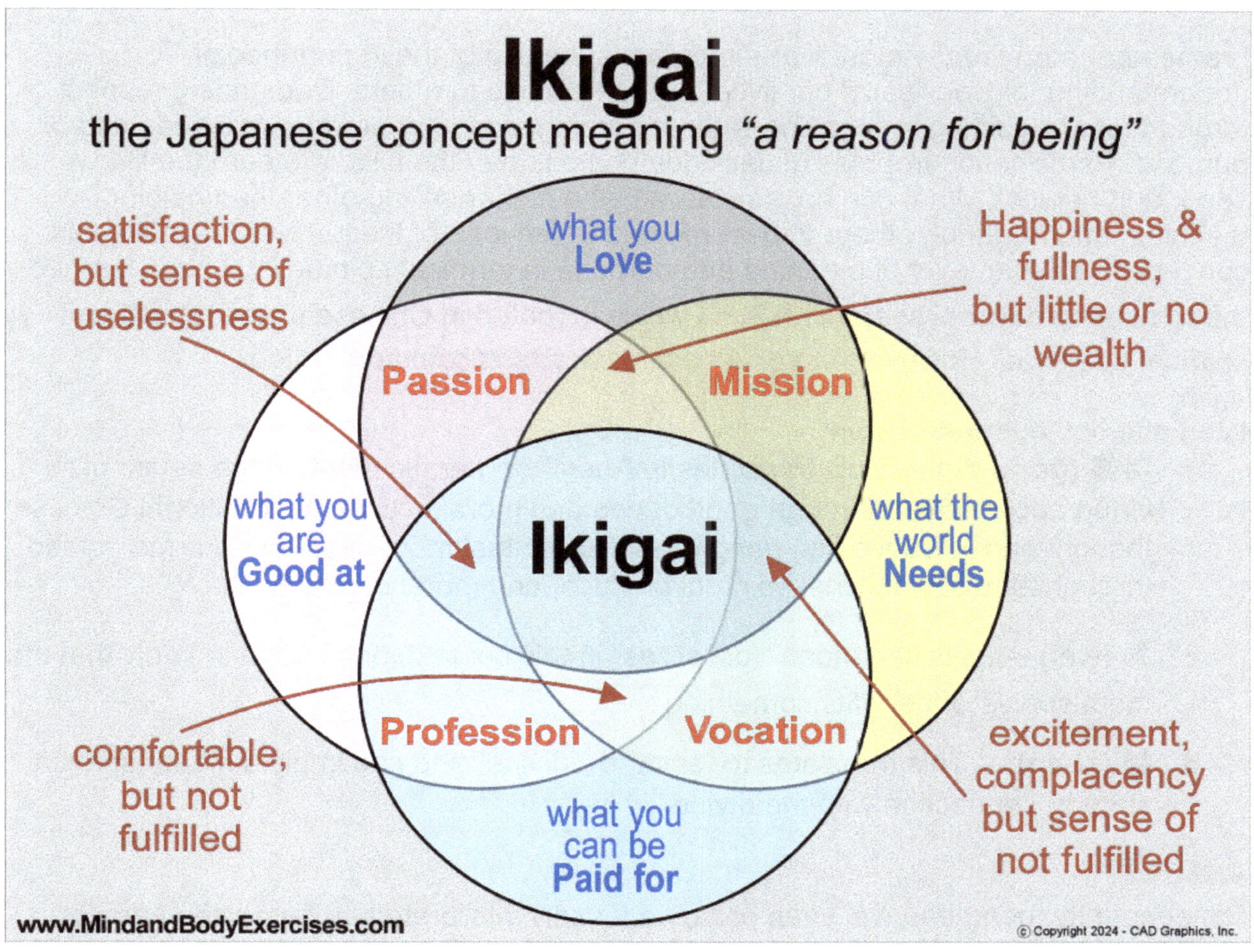

Ikigai is a Japanese concept representing the pursuit of balance among purpose, meaning, self-awareness, and self-realization (PMSS). It's the harmony of these elements that leads to a fulfilling life, especially when one's work aligns with them. Often referred to as finding one's bliss, calling, or *"inner genius,"* the four elements of PMSS are interrelated yet unique. Together, they give us a reason to get out of bed each day, guiding our lives and enriching our connections to others. Without these components, people often face a life of confusion, chaos, pain, and even a sense of emptiness and perhaps suffering.

Historically, career choice has often shaped a person's identity, with individuals feeling invisible or inadequate when career titles are lost, changed, or remain unachieved. This pressure is intensified in American culture, where respect is frequently tied to socioeconomic status, adding to the struggle of those who may feel disconnected from their purpose. Many Americans experience a lack of purpose and meaning, often heightened in later life stages. Retirees, for instance, may struggle to redefine themselves when they leave careers that once framed their identities, impacting their sense of place at home and in family life. Similarly, losing a spouse or loved one can erode this sense of purpose. For some, volunteering or public service becomes a way to revive their meaning and direction.

I remember many of my martial arts mentors speaking of the importance of understanding that we "earn" our lives through service to others. Demanding respect through fear or gaining recognition without earning, does not produce true meaning or purpose. Participation trophies usually don't help to pay the bills. We earn the life we till, seed, and harvest. What can be considered as a higher calling other than helping, teaching, and nurturing others to become better versions of themselves? To take this concept to another level of meaning and purpose in terms of spirituality, I have learned the term gong dao wei shen (功德为神) which is rooted in Chinese philosophical and spiritual traditions. However, the exact expression isn't commonly cited.

I can attempt to break it down:

1. **功德 (gong de)** — This translates to "merit" or "karmic merit" in the sense of virtue accumulated through good deeds and moral actions. In traditional Chinese thought and in Buddhism, *gong de* is the spiritual merit or positive karma gained through altruistic actions, spiritual practice, and moral conduct.

2. **为 (wei)** — This can mean "for" or "as" in this context, often used to imply that the merit serves or benefits something.

3. **神 (shen)** — This translates to "spirit" or "divine" and can imply a higher spiritual state or connection with the divine.

功德 为 神

Consequently, *gong dao wei shen* could be loosely interpreted as "*acquiring karmic merit for spiritual elevation or connection to the divine.*" This phrase might not appear in ancient texts directly but reflects the concept of dedicating good deeds or spiritual work to elevate one's spiritual state, aligning with Chinese philosophies of moral virtue impacting one's spiritual development.

Grasping these aspects of PMSS early on benefits not only individuals but also communities and society as a whole. However, finding this balance isn't something that can be bought or easily read about; it takes time, life experiences, a genuine desire, and self-reflection to develop. In this way, one's personal sense of ikigai or PMSS truly takes shape through a lifelong journey of discovery and growth.

6. The Grace of Endings

A Reflection on Relationships, Impermanence, and the Wisdom of Final Chapters
I have lived long enough, to see many of my personal relationships come to an end. Relationships with family, friends and neighbors. Also, in the workplace, or with casual acquaintances and even with most beloved pets. There is no way to escape the fact that all of our relationships,... good, bad or otherwise... will eventually wind down and consequently, ... cease to exist.

Some relationships ended gently, like the fading of a season. Some ended abruptly, with sharp edges and unfinished words. Others dissolved so slowly that I did not recognize their ending until much later. Some lasted for only seconds as meaningful encounters, while others have lasted for decades, ranging from superficial to those with much depth and connection.

A few were taken from me through death, reminding me that time is not something we negotiate.

If there is one truth I now accept without resistance, it is this: every relationship ends. The only uncertainty is how.

All Relationships End — But Not All Endings Are Equal
A relationship can end in many ways:

- Physical separation

- Emotional drifting
- Conflict or betrayal
- Mutual completion
- Growth in different directions
- Death

The ending is inevitable. The quality of the ending, however, is not. Two relationships can last the same number of years. One ends with resentment, bitterness, and silence. The other ends in gratitude, dignity, and respect. Same duration, but very different legacies. And legacy is what remains when presence is gone.

When I was younger, I assumed continuity. Friendships felt permanent. Partnerships felt anchored. Mentorships felt enduring. Even conflict seemed temporary. I moved through life with the quiet belief that what was present would remain.

Age has corrected that assumption.

In both Buddhism and Taoism, impermanence is not considered tragic; it is considered structural. Everything that arises eventually passes. Seasons change. Roles evolve. Bodies age. The river moves forward regardless of how tightly we grip the bank.

Relationships are no exception. This realization is not cynical. However, it is clarifying.

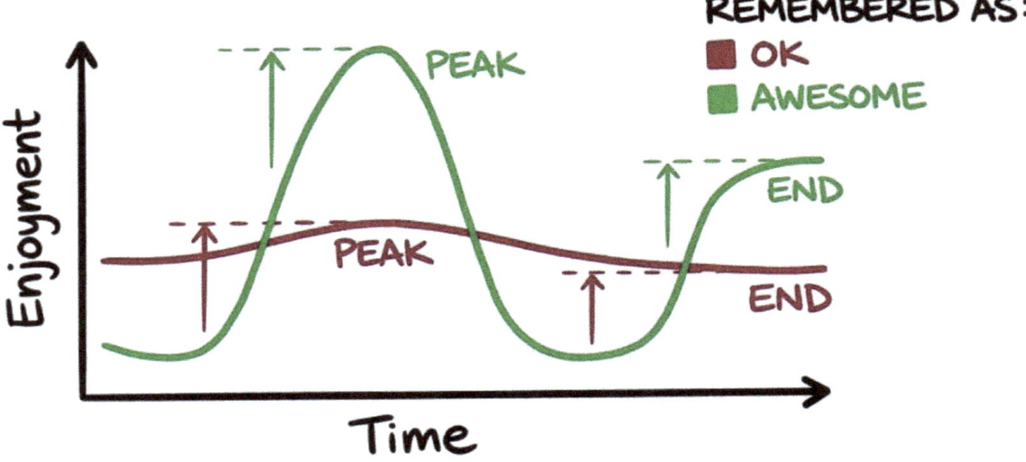

What I have come to understand is that while every relationship will end, not every ending carries the same weight. The way something concludes often determines how it is remembered. Behavioral science supports this idea through what is known as the peak–end rule, a concept associated with Daniel Kahneman. Human beings tend to remember experiences not by averaging every moment, but by recalling emotional peaks and how the experience ended.

In my own life, I have seen this play out repeatedly. Some relationships ended in mutual respect. Those I remember with gratitude, even if sadness accompanied the goodbye. Other endings were strained or unresolved. In those cases, the final chapter colored the memory of the entire story. Not because the good years disappeared, but because the emotional signature shifted.

The ending becomes a lens. Over time, I stopped asking whether a relationship lasted "long enough." Instead, I began asking whether I conducted myself well when it mattered most. Did I speak truthfully but without cruelty? Did I take responsibility for my part? Did I protect confidence even when I was hurt? Did I leave with dignity?

Ending well does not mean avoiding hard conversations. It does not mean suppressing disappointment or pretending harm did not occur. It means refusing to allow bitterness to become part of one's identity. It means honoring what was real, even if it cannot continue.

Not All Endings Are Mutual

Here is where the idea becomes more nuanced.

Sometimes:

- One person wants to leave.
- One person is hurt.
- One person feels betrayed.

The closing of a relationship is not always evenly distributed. One may feel relief while the other feels loss. One may feel clarity while the other feels confusion.

We cannot control how another person chooses to exit. But we can control whether we exit with integrity.

Not all of my endings were graceful. I have spoken too quickly at times. I have clung when I should have released. I have walked away when I should have stayed. But even the painful endings became teachers. Each one revealed something about attachment, ego, expectation, and fear.

Not all relationships are meant to last.
Some are teachers.
Some are mirrors.
Some are initiations.
Some are seasonal.
But how we exit determines whether the experience becomes:

- Trauma
- Bitterness
- Or growth

Each one forced me to refine who I was.

If I have gained anything from the relationships that have ended — well or poorly — it is perspective.

Now, as I enter what many call the golden years of life, I do not assume longevity in any relationship. I try to be present. I strive to be responsible. I presume that any conversation could be the last meaningful exchange. That awareness changes how I speak. It softens unnecessary conflict and reduces trivial ego battles. It encourages gratitude.

It also deepens intentionality.

When we recognize that every relationship has a final chapter, we begin to live differently in the earlier ones. We may express appreciation more freely. We may forgive more quickly. We can choose our words more carefully. We can protect what matters and release what does not.

Relationships do not truly end when contact stops. They continue within us. They shape habits, perspectives, and character. Some leave behind wisdom. Some leave behind warnings. Some leave behind quiet gratitude. All leave impressions.

The quality of the ending influences the emotional afterlife of the relationship.

If I could offer anything to those who are younger, it would not be advice on how to make every relationship last forever. That is not within our control. Instead, I would suggest this:

Conduct yourself in such a way that, if the relationship ended tomorrow, you would not regret your final chapter.

Try not to weaponize vulnerability. Try not to humiliate in anger. Do not rewrite history to protect pride. Do not allow ego to eclipse shared humanity.

You cannot control how others leave. But you can control how you do.

In the end, our legacy is not built upon how long relationships lasted, but upon how we treated others within them. Especially when they were ending. Dignity under pressure is remembered. Respect in conflict is remembered. Gratitude in goodbye is remembered. Every relationship will one day close. That is not a morbid thought, but rather a refining one.

Knowing this has not made me withdraw. It has made me more attentive, careful. and grateful. More willing to release without resentment.

The final chapter will come for every connection I still hold. When it does, I hope the memory left behind is steady, respectful, and honest. Not perfect, but principled.
If endings are inevitable, then grace becomes essential. And perhaps that is one of the quiet purposes of aging: to understand that relationships are not possessions to secure, but gifts to steward right up until their final page.

7. The 3 Treasures

Mind *(Qi)*– How and what you think about and how you process information from sensory input. From the Traditional Chinese Medicine TCM) perspective, the mind is related to the vitality of the breath. Responsible for the blueprint of internal and external functions of the energy force within the body. Qi can be equated to the flame which is the source of the light that illuminates from the candle. The flame eventually consumes the candle. Qi is one's energy or vitality. When Qi is used wisely, one's Jing can last longer. Qi is lost through regular daily activities but gained back through good habits of diet, exercise, breathing, and sleep.

Body *(Jing)* – The physical matter that makes up you and how well it functions. The physical structure of the body's tissue. Responsible for the developmental processes of the body. Jing can be equated to the wick and the wax which is the fuel for the source of the flame. Better quality wax determines the longevity of the candle. One's Jing is determined by genetic inheritance. Jing is depleted over one's lifetime and is not easily replenished.

Spirit *(Shen)* – What you believe as far as beliefs in the unknown, faith, morals, a purpose, etc. The refined level of the mind and higher consciousness. Consists of the spirit, soul, and mind. Responsible for the interaction of destiny & fate. Maintains internal and external functions. Shen can be equated to the light that illuminates a candle. The candle's purpose is to light the darkness. One's Shen is the illumination of their spirit. When one's Jing and Qi are in abundance, Shen is released. Shen is divided further into the mind (shen), the intellect (yi), the corporeal soul (po), willpower (zhi) and the ethereal soul (hun). These 5 shen are a topic for another discussion.

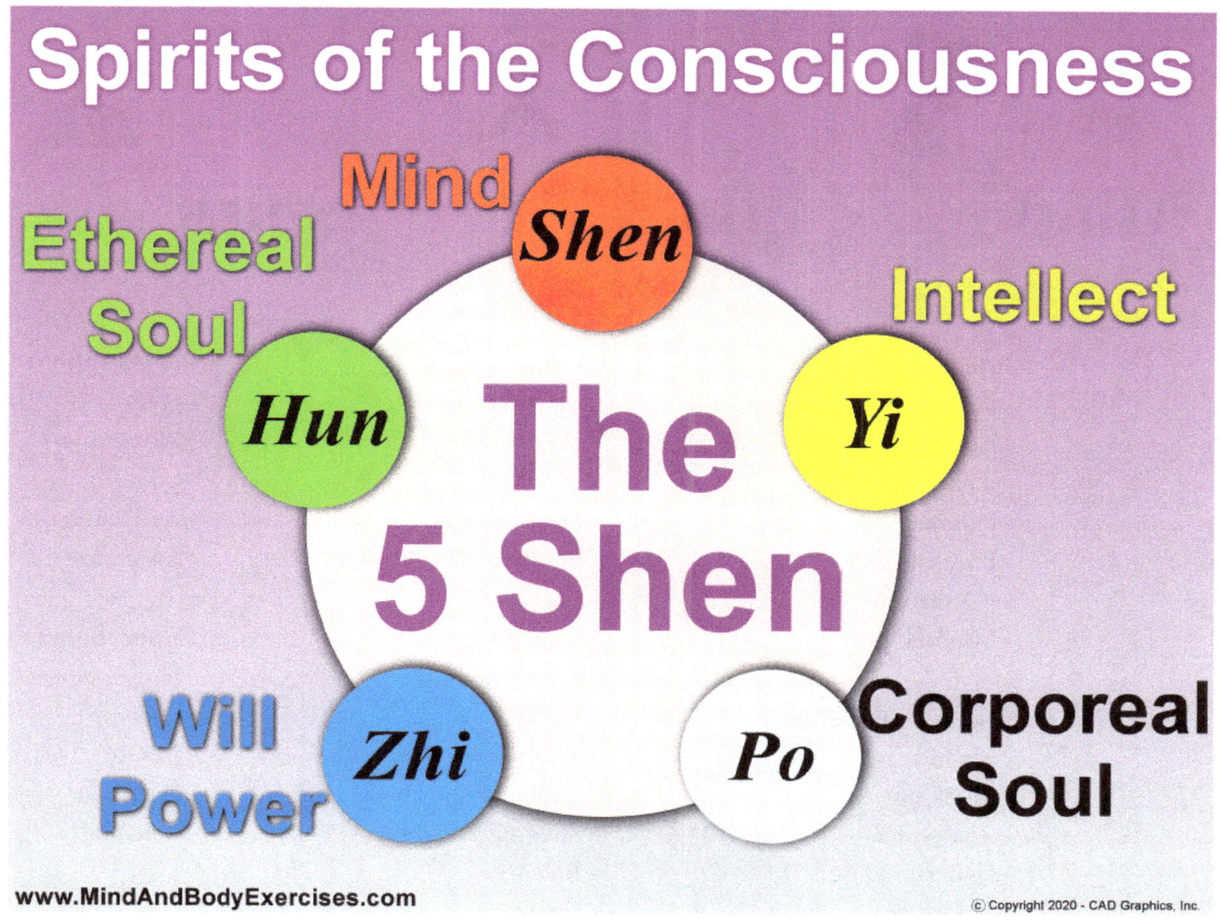

These three treasures are the most valuable things that we all possess. Without these 3, we have no family, no friends, no career, no big house, no internet. What we sometimes see today as “new” is indeed rather old. This concept of the 3 Treasures comes from Taoism, a philosophy that is over 2000 years old, originating around 500 BCE. These are universal truths that are hard to debate. We all need to take care of our own “treasures” before we can be of benefit to those around us. Breathe deeper, exercise more, eat better, and earn a good night’s sleep by being active and relieving stress during the day.

Modern science and research seek to label and dissect any and all things, intending to assign a name or label to all that *is* and sometimes that which *is not*. With this realization, we can see from the graphic below the many sub-categories that are now thought to be parts of the original concept of mind, body, and spirit.

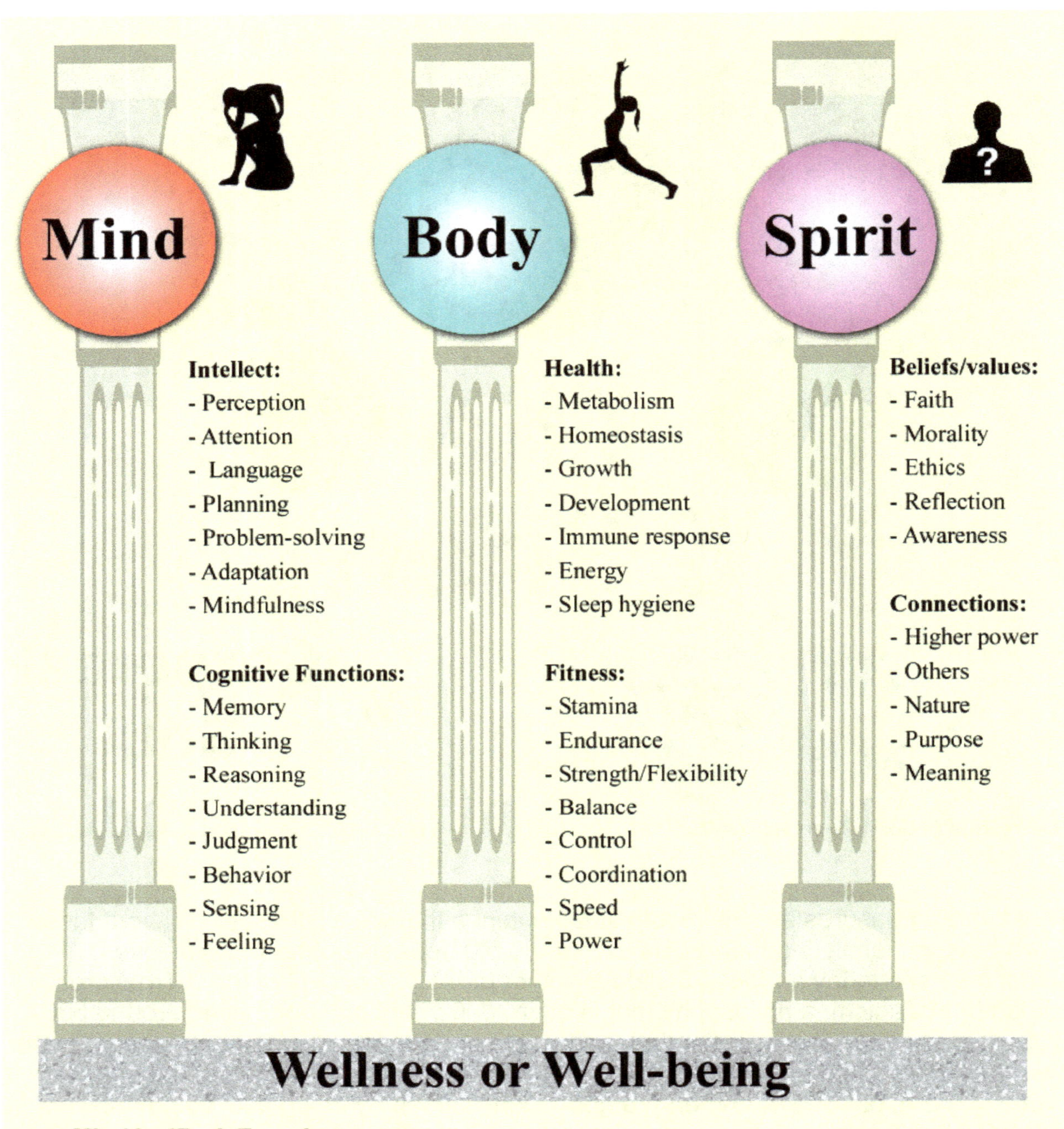
Mind
Body
Spirit
?
Intellect:
- Perception
- Attention
- Language
- Planning
- Problem-solving
- Adaptation
- Mindfulness
Cognitive Functions:
- Memory
- Thinking
- Reasoning
- Understanding
- Judgment
- Behavior
- Sensing
- Feeling
Health:
- Metabolism
- Homeostasis
- Growth
- Development
- Immune response
- Energy
- Sleep hygiene
Fitness:
- Stamina
- Endurance
- Strength/Flexibility
- Balance
- Control
- Coordination
- Speed
- Power
Beliefs/values:
- Faith
- Morality
- Ethics
- Reflection
- Awareness
Connections:
- Higher power
- Others
- Nature
- Purpose
- Meaning
Wellness or Well-being
www.MindAndBodyExercises.com
ⓒ Copyright 2024 - CAD Graphics, Inc.

The mind is comprised of various components:
Intellect:

- Perception – recognizing and acknowledging sensory stimuli.
- Attention – ability to focus on specific thoughts and stimuli.
- Language – understanding and producing speech and writing.
- Planning – ability to formulate a strategy or process.
- Problem-solving – finding solutions to complex issues.
- Decision-making – making choices among options.
- Adaptation – being able to change and adjust thoughts, feelings, and actions.
- Mindfulness – an awareness of current thoughts, feelings, and surroundings.

Cognitive Functions:

- Memory – storage and retrieval of information.
- Thinking – the mental process of considering or reasoning about something.
- Reasoning – the process of drawing conclusions or making inferences based on evidence and logical principles.
- Understanding – to comprehend the meaning or significance of something.
- Judgment – the ability to make considered decisions or come to sensible conclusions.
- Behavior – the actions or reactions of an individual in response to external or internal stimuli.
- Sensing – the process of detecting and responding to stimuli through the sensory organs.
- Feelings – experiences of emotions.

The body can be broken down into various categories:
Health:

- Metabolism – chemical processes that occur within living organisms.
- Homeostasis – the body's ability to manage and regulate stable internal bodily functions and conditions.
- Growth/development – physical changes throughout a living organism's lifespan.
- Immune response – ability of the body to defend against pathogens.
- Energy – the amount of physical power that can be drawn upon.

- Sleep hygiene – the quality of an individual's ability to rest and recover.

Fitness:

- Survival – on the most basic level, the ability to stay alive.
- Stamina – ability to sustain prolonged physical for an extended time without fatigue.
- Endurance – the muscular system's capacity to sustain activity.
- Strength – the ability of muscles to exert force against resistance
- Flexibility – the range of motion available at a joint or group of joints
- Balance – the ability to maintain the body's position, whether stationary or while moving.
- Control – to manage and direct the body's movements precisely and efficiently.
- Coordination – ability to use different parts of the body together smoothly and efficiently.
- Speed – to move quickly across the ground or move limbs rapidly for a specific purpose.
- Power – ability to exert maximum force in the shortest amount of time.

Spirit can be interpreted through numerous facets:
Beliefs/values:

- Faith – belief in principles of an organized religion or spiritual practice.
- Morality – the ability to differentiate between what is considered right and wrong.
- Ethics – a system of moral principles.
- Reflection – the ability to be aware of one's own thoughts and actions.
- Awareness – a sense of one's self, surroundings, and relative environment.

Connections:

- Higher power – a sense of a greater presence beyond themselves.
- Others – relationships with people, and community.
- Nature – relationships with all living creatures and the environment.
- Purpose – a reason to wake up every day.
- Meaning – realization of one's reason for existing

8. Three Treasures plus Emptiness

In Taoist cultivation theory, the "Three Treasures" (*sān bǎo*) of *jīng, qì* and *shén* describe successive refinements of being: from bodily substance to energy to spirit. Alongside and underpinning this transformative process is the principle of *xū*, often translated "emptiness", "void", or "hollow openness". Xū is not mere nothingness, but a dynamic receptive ground that allows emergence, transformation, and return. This essay explicates the meaning of xū, its relation to the Three Treasures, and how classical Taoist texts articulate this interplay.

The Three Treasures: Jīng, Qì and Shén
The Three Treasures are central in Taoist internal alchemy (*nèi dān*) as the raw materials and vehicles of transformation.

Treasure	Chinese	Key meaning	Role in cultivation
Essence	精 (*jīng*)	The dense, material-vital substance (including inherited vitality, reproductive substance) (Bartek, 2024)	Reserved, refined and conserved; the "root" of life and alchemical process.
Vital energy / breath	氣 (*qì*)	The dynamic life-force, movement, breath, transformation of substance into energy (Bartek, 2024)	Circulates, refines essence into spirit; bridges body and spirit.
Spirit / consciousness	神 (*shén*)	The refined, luminous aspect of awareness, spirit, mind, divine seed (Pregadio, 2009)	The outcome of refinement; the luminous presence and the vehicle of transcendence.

In internal-alchemy texts such as the Wuzhen Pian attributed to Zhang Boduan, the Three Treasures are explicitly cited as the ingredients of the internal elixir:

"…the body contains the essential components: these Three Treasures are jīng, qì and shén."

Thus, the alchemist's work is to refine jīng → qì → shén and finally to integrate with the Way (道).

The Concept of Xū

Definition and nuance
The Chinese character 虛 (*xū*) conveys "emptiness", "voidness", "hollowness", "open space", "vacancy", but importantly also "receptivity", "openness", "ungrasped potential". In Taoist texts, xū is often the invisible space or still ground that allows form, movement, being, and return.

For example, in the classic Tao Te Ching by Laozi, Chapter 11 states:

"Thirty spokes join at one hub; it is the emptiness (xū) that makes the wagon useful. Cast clay into a vessel; it is the emptiness inside that makes it useful. Cut out doors and windows to make a room; it is the emptiness within that makes it inhabitable." (Tao Te Ching by Lao Tzu – Verse 11 – Three Translations, 2021)

And Chapter 16:

*"Attain complete emptiness (xū); hold fast to stillness. The myriad beings arise - yet each returns to its root." (*Tao Te Ching by Lao Tzu – Verse 11 – Three Translations, 2021)

Thus xū is both origin and destination. It is the silent ground from which being arises and to which it returns.

Xū in internal alchemy
In internal alchemy (nèi dān), xū becomes the "vessel" or "cauldron" within the practitioner, as an inner space, body-mind field of openness, into which essence, energy and spirit are guided. According to scholarship:

> *"In meditative practices, they visualize the human body as a cauldron that refines the internal vital forces including essence (jīng), pneuma (qì), and spirit (shén) to produce an internal elixir..."* (Wuzhen Pian 悟真篇 Also Known as "Essay on the [Immediate] Awakening to Truth", "Chapters on Awakening to Perfection" - UBC Library Open Collections, n.d.)

Also:
"It regards humans as a set of tripods and stoves for refining and enhancing one's own life energy (jīng, qì, shén) ... The first stage involves replenishing jīng, qì and shén, ... the final is returning to emptiness." (Golden Elixir Press, n.d.)

Hence, xū is the operative "space" in which the refinement jīng → qì → shén occurs, and into which shén finally dissolves.

Relationship of Xū to the Three Treasures

Here is how xū operates at each stage of the alchemical process:

Transformation stage	Role of Xū	Implication for cultivation
jīng → qì	The practitioner first quiets distractions, reserves essence, cultivates stillness—creating an inner emptiness (xū) so that jīng does not scatter.	Cultivating "emptied receptivity": less sensory input, fewer desires, conserving jīng.
qì → shén	Energy (qì) flows within the "empty vessel" (xū), unimpeded by conceptual/motional turbulence; this allows qì to transform into shén.	Cultivation shifts to subtle awareness, opening to spirit, refining vital energy in the void.
shén → Return to Xū	At completion, the refined shén merges into emptiness (xū), dissolving the individual self into universal ground (道). The Three Treasures originate from xū and return to xū.	The goal: abiding in xū as "Spirit and Emptiness united as one".

In other words:
xū is neither an added "fourth treasure" nor merely an absence, but the field of transformation and integration of the Three Treasures. Without xū: jīng stagnates, qì scatters, shén remains bound. With xū: alchemy is possible, transformation flows, transcendence becomes attainable.

Classical Source Quotations

Here are selected quotations with Chinese original and annotated translation:

1. From Tao Te Ching, Ch. 11
   - *"Thirty spokes join at one hub; yet it is the emptiness therein that gives the wheel its use. Kneading clay to form a vessel; yet it is the emptiness therein that makes the vessel useful…"* (Dao De Jing [Tao Te Ching], by Lao Zi [Lao Tzu] in Side-by-Side Translation: Chapter 11, n.d.)

2. From Tao Te Ching, Ch. 16
   - *"Attain complete emptiness; hold fast to stillness. The myriad beings all arise - I watch their return. The myriad things flourish and each returns to its root. Returning to the root is called stillness. Stillness is called returning to destiny. Returning to destiny is called the Constant. Knowing the Constant is called clarity…"* (Garofalo, n.d.)

3. From Wuzhen Pian

    - Though specific lines are metaphorical and sparse, one commentary notes: *"The body contains the essential components. These Three Treasures are jīng, qì and shén."* (Wikipedia contributors, 2025)
    - And that this text visualizes the human body as a cauldron refining the Three Treasures. (Wuzhen Pian 悟真篇 Also Known as "Essay on the [Immediate] Awakening to Truth", "Chapters on Awakening to Perfection" - UBC Library Open Collections, n.d.)

4. Scholarly exegesis: *"The first stage involves replenishing essence, breath and spirit … and the final is returning to emptiness."* (Golden Elixir Press, n.d.)
5. Interpretation of the Three Treasures in Chinese culture: *"The ancient Daoists believed that man exists inseparably between heaven and earth and that there is a mutual relationship between these three (heaven, earth, man) …"* in relation to jīng, qì, shén. (Bartek, 2024)

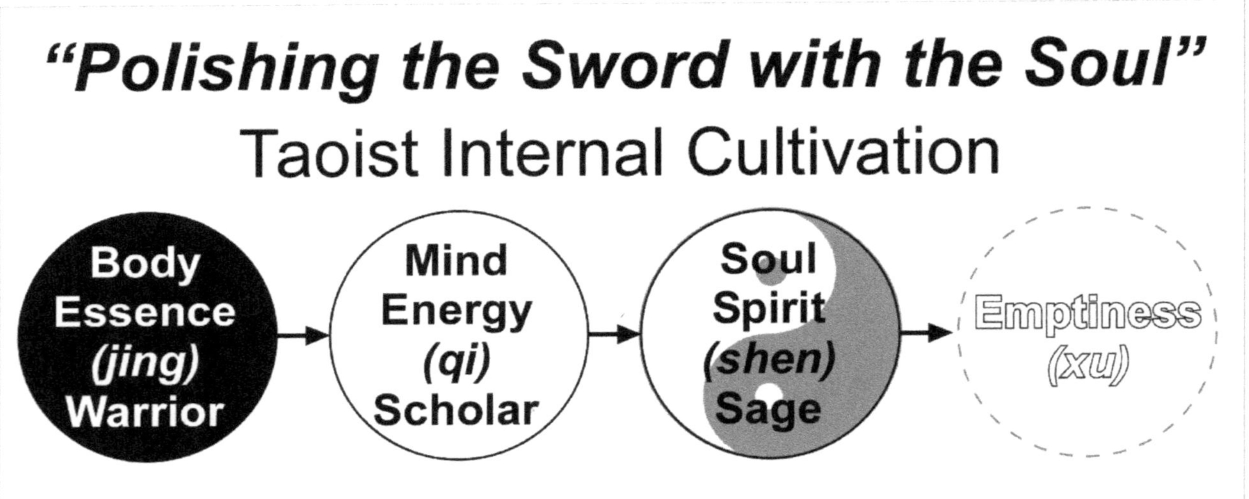

Summary

- The Three Treasures (jīng, qì, shén) chart an inner alchemical journey: the body's essence → refined energy → luminous spirit.
- Xū (emptiness) is not a fourth treasure but the primordial field within which the alchemical transformation occurs and to which it ultimately returns.
- Cultivation involves first creating receptivity and emptiness (xū) to conserve essence, then refining energy in the vessel of emptiness, and finally abiding in emptiness as spirit dissolves into the Way.
- The classical Taoist tradition (via Laozi's Tao Te Ching and texts like Wuzhen Pian) illustrates this with metaphors of wheel hubs, vessels, cauldrons, and return to root.

- Practically, meditation and Qigong aim to “clear the vessel”, “quiet the hub”, “walk the empty path” so that the Three Treasures can operate in harmony.

References

Bartek. (2024, June 28). *Jing, Qi, Shen – Die drei Schätze*. Path of Dao. https://path-of-dao-qigong.ch/en/jing-qi-shen/

Dao De Jing [Tao Te ching], by Lao Zi [Lao Tzu] in Side-by-Side Translation: Chapter 11. (n.d.). YellowBridge. https://www.yellowbridge.com/onlinelit/daodejing11.php?utm_source=chatgpt.com

Garofalo, M. P. (n.d.). *Dao de Jing, Laozi, Chapter 16*. https://mpgtaijiquan.blogspot.com/2015/05/dao-de-jing-laozi-chapter-16.html?utm_source=chatgpt.com

Golden Elixir Press. (n.d.). *Foundations of Internal Alchemy — A slideshow*. Scribd. https://www.scribd.com/document/99535352/Foundations-of-Internal-Alchemy-A-Slideshow?utm_source=chatgpt.com

Pregadio, F. (2009). Awakening to Reality: The “Regulated Verses” of the Wuzhen pian, a Taoist Classic of Internal Alchemy. In *Golden Elixir Press*. https://www.goldenelixir.com/files/Introduction_to_Awakening_to_Reality.pdf?utm_source=chatgpt.com

The Project Gutenberg eBook of *Dao de Jing*, by Lao Zi. (n.d.). https://www.gutenberg.org/files/49965/49965-h/49965-h.htm?utm_source=chatgpt.com

Tao Te Ching by Lao Tzu – Verse 11 – Three translations. (2021, November 30). Vishy’s Blog. https://vishytheknight.wordpress.com/2021/11/30/tao-te-ching-by-lao-tzu-verse-11-three-translations/?utm_source=chatgpt.com

Wikipedia contributors. (2025, October 1). Wuzhen pian. Wikipedia. https://en.wikipedia.org/wiki/Wuzhen_pian?utm_source=chatgpt.com

Wuzhen pian 悟真篇 also known as “Essay on the [Immediate] Awakening to Truth”, “Chapters on Awakening to Perfection” - UBC Library Open Collections. (n.d.). https://open.library.ubc.ca/cIRcle/collections/ubccommunityandpartnerspublicati/52387/items/1.0416054?utm_source=chatgpt.com

9. Four-Phase Expansion of the Jing–Qi–Shen Developmental Model

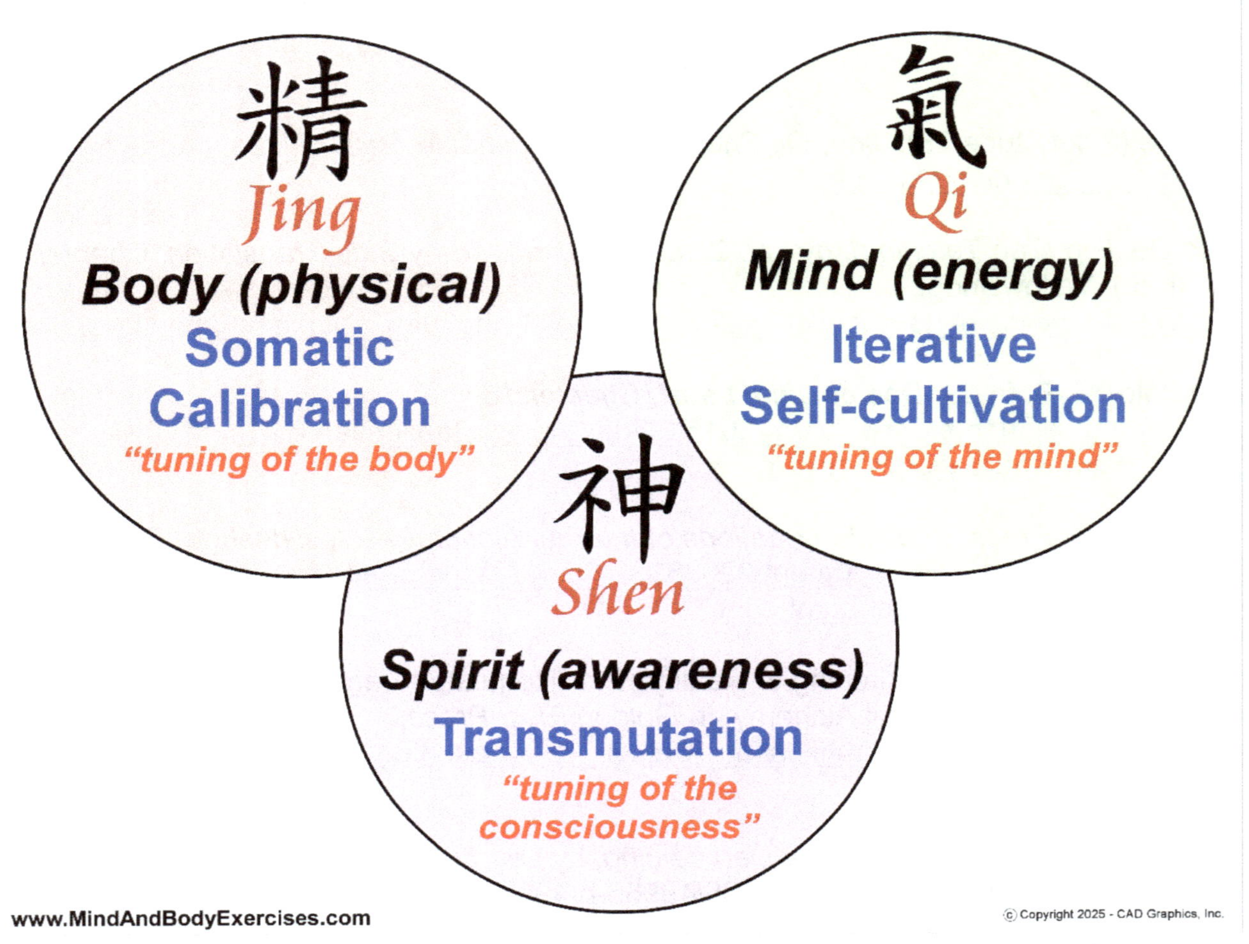

Phase 1 — Foundational Awareness: Somatic Calibration (Jing)
Phase 1 represents the foundational stage where the practitioner learns to attune their physical body, **the *Jing* level,** through heightened somatic awareness and physiological regulation. At this level, the focus is on:

- **Interoception:** sensing internal signals such as breath, heartbeat, and muscular tension
- **Proprioception:** detecting body position and micro-adjustments
- **Regulatory Responsiveness:** adjusting posture, breathing, and alignment

Somatic calibration stabilizes the "*base material*" of the human system. In Taoist internal arts, this is the earliest refinement of Jing: raw essence becoming cleaner, clearer, and more governable.

Neuroscientifically, this phase strengthens communication between the insula (interoceptive awareness), anterior cingulate cortex (attention and motivation), and prefrontal cortex (regulation and decision-making). When these systems integrate, the practitioner becomes capable of sensing imbalances long before they erupt into dysfunction (Khalsa et al., 2018).

This phase is therefore concerned with:

- Cultivating *"felt sense"*
- Stabilizing the nervous system
- Learning to *"hear"* the body
- Establishing physical coherence

Without Phase 1, progression into deeper phases becomes imbalanced or potentially unsafe.

This is the **Jing → stability** transformation.

Phase 2 — Cyclical Refinement: Iterative Self-cultivation (Qi)
Once somatic clarity is established, the practitioner advances toward the mental-energetic domain, **the *Qi* level**. This phase introduces iterative practice and self-correction, forming the living engine of personal development.
Here, the operating principle is **iteration**:

Practice → feedback → correction → integration → renewed practice

Across martial arts, meditation, and qigong lineages, this cyclical refinement is recognized as **gongfu (kung fu),** not mere skill, but the cultivated discipline earned through dedicated repetition. Each iteration reshapes:

- Motor pathways
- Emotional patterns
- Cognitive habits
- Energetic circulation

Modern neuroscience parallels this with **experience-dependent neuroplasticity** or the gradual restructuring of brain networks for resilience, emotional regulation, and attentional stability (Davidson & McEwen, 2012).

Spiritually and philosophically, Phase 2 is where one begins forging ***de*** (virtue, cultivated inner power). The practitioner transitions from merely *feeling* the body to *shaping* the self.

At this stage, Qi becomes more coherent and directed. Mental habits are tuned, intentions sharpen, and discipline becomes embodied.

This is the **Qi → refinement** transformation.

Phase 3 — Synthetic Integration: Transmutation (Shen)
Phase 3 transitions from refinement into **whole-system synthesis**, corresponding to the ***Shen* level,** with awareness, meaning, and inner illumination.

Here the practitioner no longer simply adjusts the body (Phase 1) or trains the mind through iteration (Phase 2). Instead, they **convert base tendencies into higher capacities**. This includes:

- fear → insight
- pain → empathy
- discipline → wisdom
- adversity → meaning

This is the essence of **transmutation** in internal alchemy (neidan):

Jing → Qi → Shen → back to emptiness and clarity

Physiologically, this level parallels harmonization of endocrine rhythms, autonomic coherence, and emotional centers that once produced reactivity but now produce calm presence.
Psychologically, the practitioner embodies authenticity rather than performance. Their presence becomes stabilizing to others, as they can become “the light that guides.”
Phase 3 is where:

- the body listens
- the mind learns
- *consciousness reorients* toward clarity

This is the **Shen → illumination** transformation.

Bring it all together - the Harmonization (Integration of Jing–Qi–Shen)
My diagrams and progression of images naturally imply a fourth phase, which is the integrative stage where Jing, Qi, and Shen no longer operate as separate domains but revolve in a recursive living spiral.
Here, the practitioner reaches a point where:

- Somatic calibration is continuous and automatic
- Iterative self-cultivation is self-initiating
- Transmutation becomes a way of life

- All three influence each other simultaneously

This is the phase where the *circle completes itself yet continues upward,* a spiral path rather than a linear one.

In this 4th Phase the practitioner embodies:

1. **Physical alignment (Jing)**
   Effortless posture, efficient movement, regulated physiology.

2. **Mental clarity and energetic coherence (Qi)**
   Stable attention, balanced emotions, refined intentions.

3. **Spiritual awareness (Shen)**
   Insight, compassion, spaciousness, wisdom.

4. **Harmonized integration**
   The practitioner is no longer "performing techniques" as
   they have become the technique.

This is the lived outcome of the entire model of the *Warrior, Scholar* and *Sage*:

Somatic Calibration → Iterative Self-cultivation → Transmutation → Integrated Being.

How the Four Phases Correspond to my Diagrams (Stages 1–4)

Stage 1 (Jing/Qi/Shen circles):
Introduces the classical triad, three aspects as separate yet related.

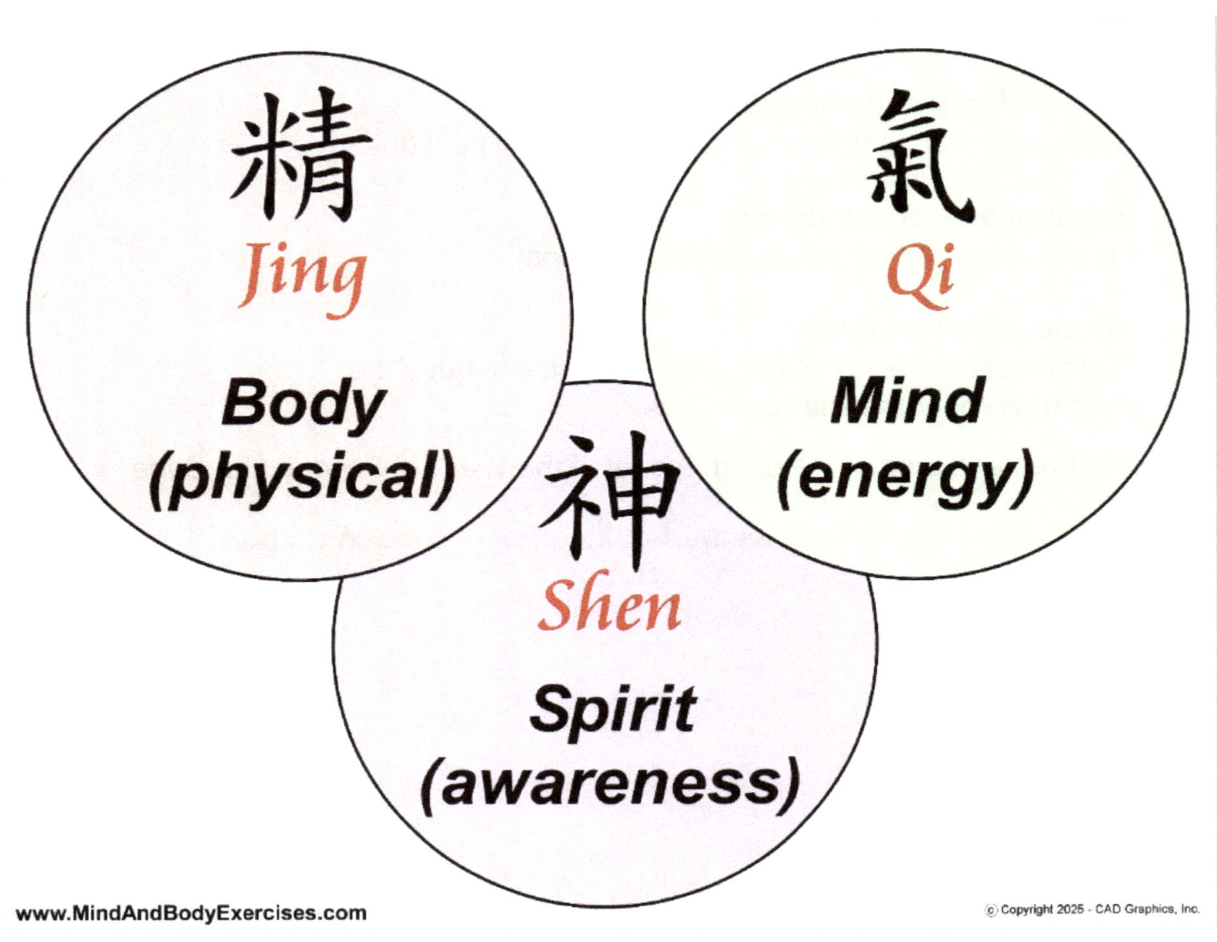

Stage 2 (Physiology/Psychology/Philosophy overlay):
Connects each classical aspect with modern disciplines.

This becomes the foundation of Phase 1.

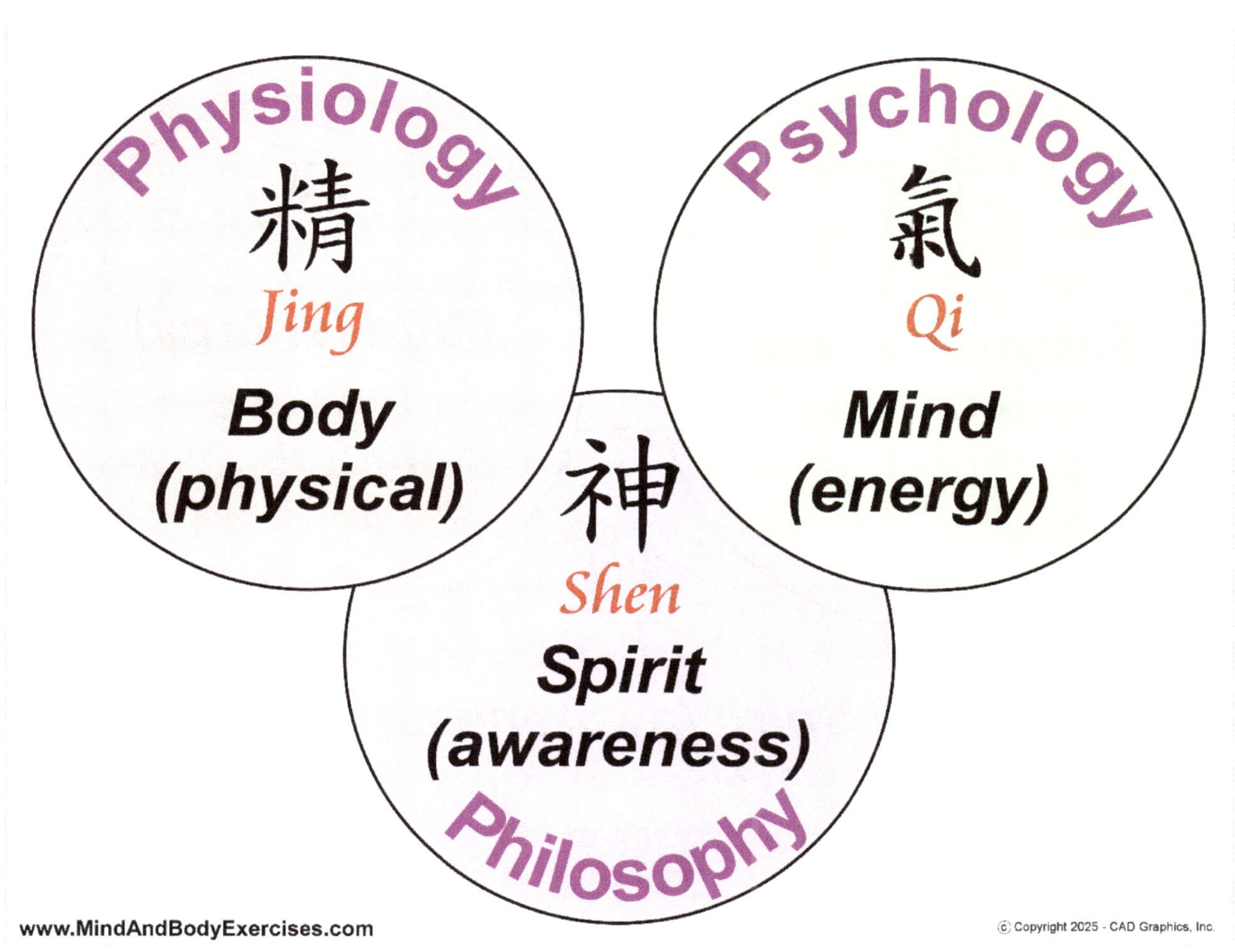

Stage 3 (Somatic Calibration / Iterative Self-cultivation / Transmutation overlay): Maps each classical component into the three functional processes.

This is Phase 2 and Phase 3.

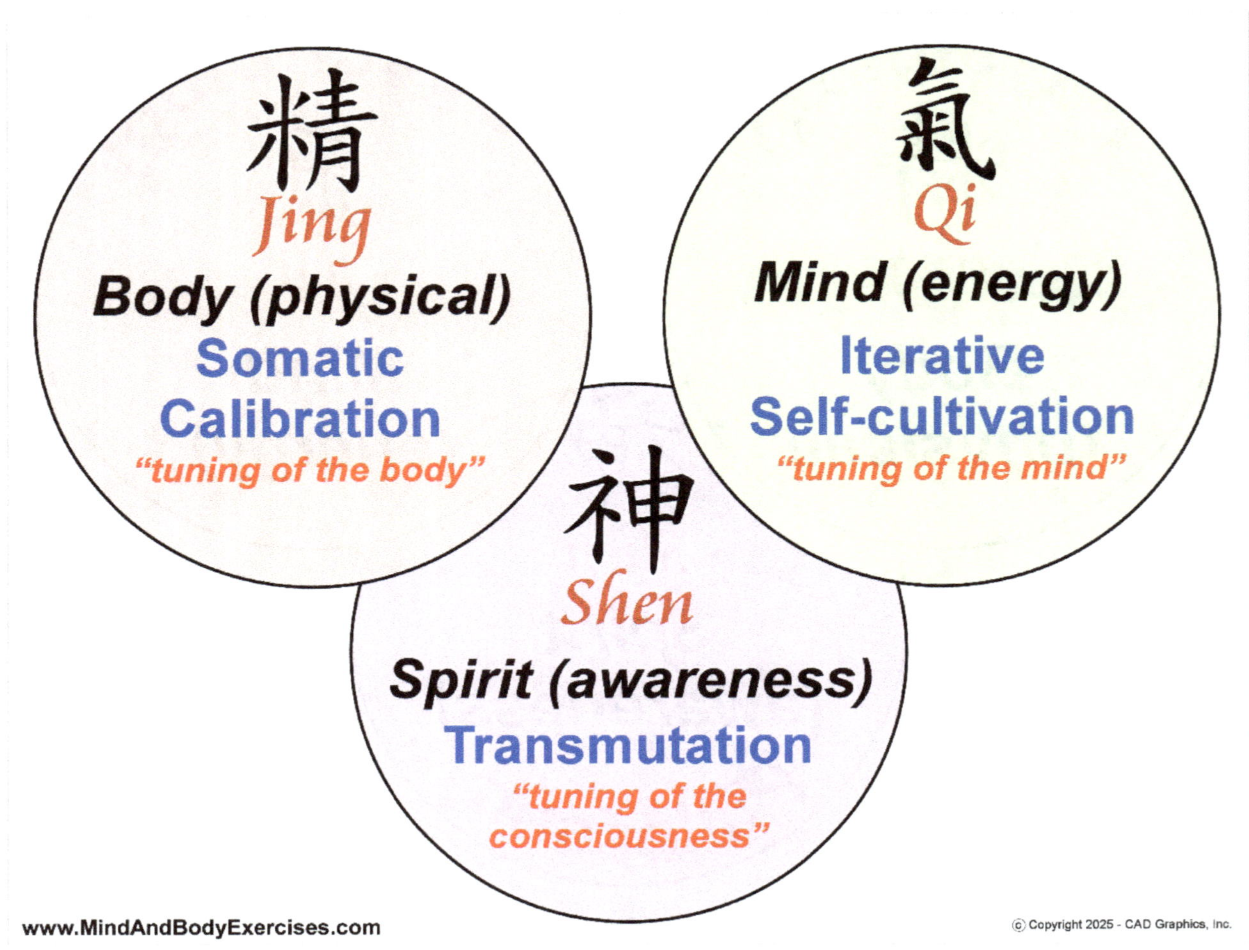

Stage 4 (Full elaborated diagram with figures):
Demonstrates the mature, embodied expression of all three components working in harmony.

This represents Phase 4.

Somatic Calibration

refines awareness and alignment

"tuning of the body"

Somatic Awareness (interoception)
consciously perceiving sensations of tension, breath, heartbeat, and alignment

Interoceptive Accuracy (cognitive processes)
the brain's interpretation of internal bodily cues

Regulatory Responsiveness (adjustments)
the capacity to modify one's physiological state, through breathing, posture, or focus to achieve balance

Iterative Self-cultivation

builds discipline and stability

"tuning of the mind"

mindful practice, reflection, and correction

the ongoing cycle of practice - feedback - adjustment - integration.

deliberate repetition that rewires synaptic pathways for stability, emotional regulation, and self-mastery

Each repetition deepens skill while gradually refining the character, much like tempering a sword through alternating heat and cooling.

Transmutation

realizes integration and illumination

"tuning of the consciousness"

the conversion of base tendencies into higher expression

Through calibrated awareness and continuous self-cultivation, internal friction and limitation become fuel for illumination

Regular engagement in mindful movement or performance retrains the nervous system to operate in coherence, balancing sympathetic activation (energy, readiness) and parasympathetic recovery (calm, restoration).

www.MindAndBodyExercises.com

Integrated Summary

- **Phase 1—Somatic Calibration:** tuning the body (Jing), establishing stability and awareness.
- **Phase 2—Iterative Self-cultivation:** tuning the mind (Qi), cultivating discipline, neuroplasticity, and virtuous habits.
- **Phase 3—Transmutation:** tuning the consciousness (Shen), converting tendencies into illumination.
- **Phase 4—Recursive Harmonization:** integrating Jing–Qi–Shen into a coherent, unified mode of being.

Together these phases describe a **complete developmental alchemical model** bridging Taoist tradition, neuroscience, psychology, and embodied martial philosophy.

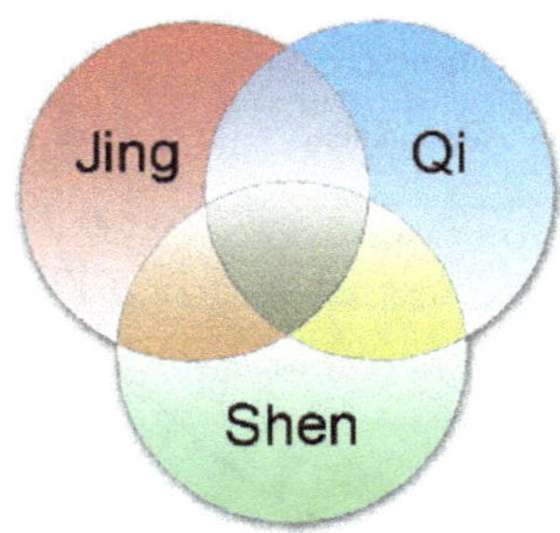

10. Taoism Viewed as a Philosophy, Vitalizing or Religious

The Chinese character for *"the Tao"*

Taoism or Daoism is based upon the concept of the *Tao (or Dao)* and its literal meaning of the *path*, or *way*. The Tao is the main principle of Taoism, where the Tao is seen as the natural order of the universe. This understanding of the universe and all-encompassing things within whether alive or inanimate cannot be defined in mere words but rather become known through actual living experience in everyday beings (Smith, 2009).

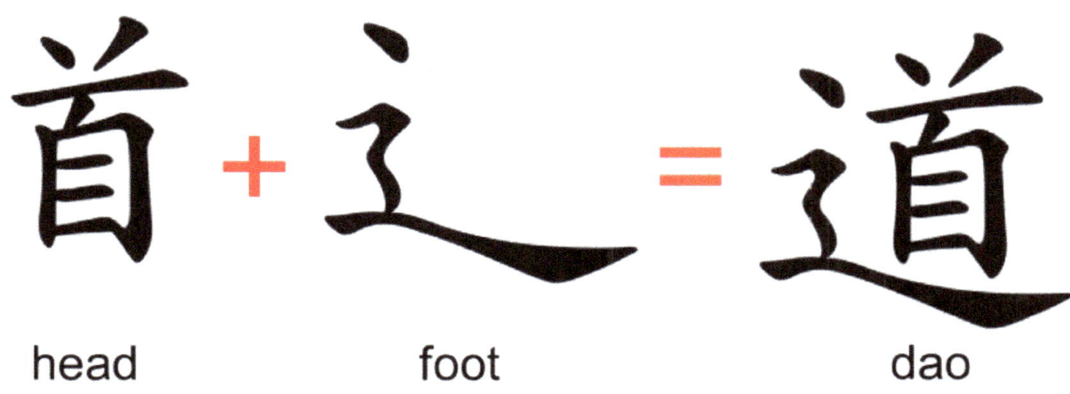

The Taoist individual becomes more reliant upon their own intuition in order to understand the potential for their own individual wisdom. The universe came into being with us together; with us, all things are one. The Tao is simply inconceivable, and therefore it is useless to say another word about it. Intuitively, we know there is a dimension of ourselves and of nature that eludes us because it is too close, too general, and too all-embracing to be singled out as a particular object. This dimension is the ground of all the astonishing forms and experiences of which we are aware. Because we are aware, it cannot be unconscious, although we are not conscious of it as an external thing. We can give it a name but cannot make any definitive statement about it. The only way of apprehending it is by watching the process and patterns of nature and by the meditative discipline of allowing our minds to become quiet, to have a vivid awareness of "what is" without verbal comment.

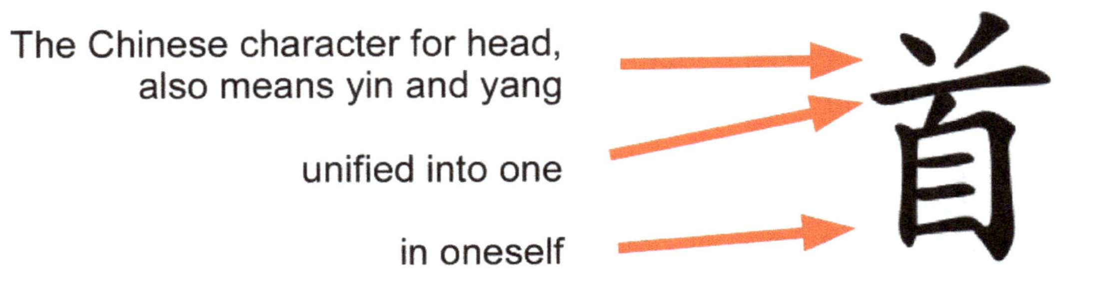

Chinese culture and its views on religion have evolved over many centuries with Confucianism, Taoism, and Buddhism being considered the "three pillars" of ancient Chinese society (National Geographic Society, 2022). Consequently, most Chinese people have practiced Confucianism in their ethics and public life, Taoism in their private life and hygiene, and Buddhism at the time of death, along with shamanistic folk religion also added in along the way. "Every Chinese wears a Confucian hat, Taoist robes, and Buddhist sandals" (Smith, 2009).

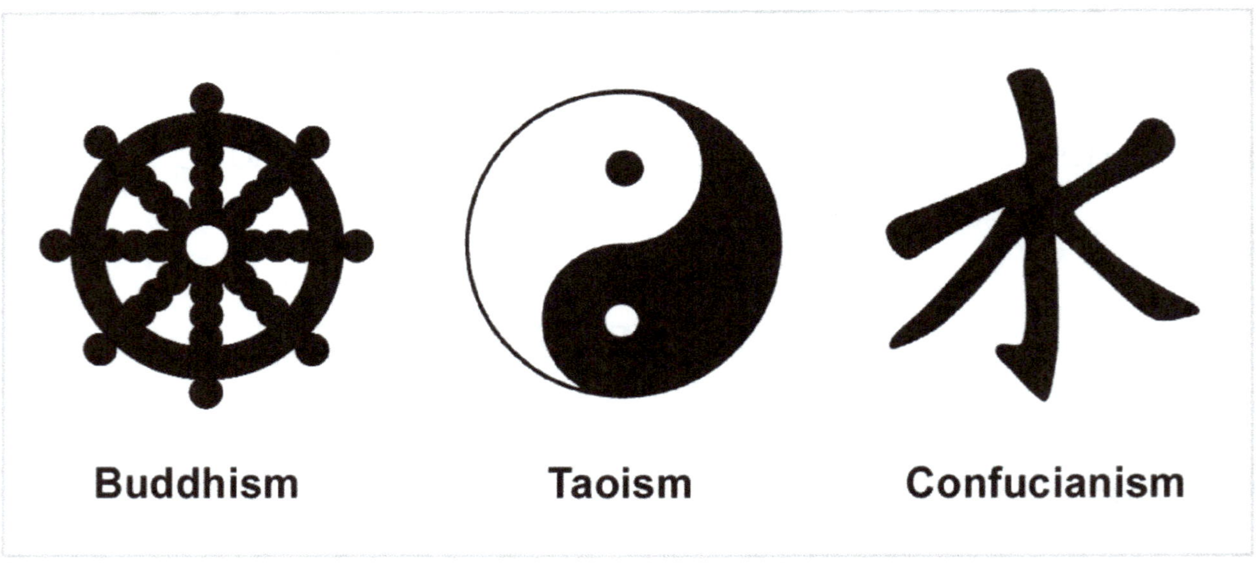

There are 3 main types of Taoism. The first type is referred to as philosophical Taoism, where it is essentially a frame of mind, where the goal is to conserve one's *te* or power, by expending it efficiently. This type of Taoism holds the main concept of *wu wei*, meaning "inaction" but in Taoism means pure effectiveness. Wu wei is an action in which the individual strives to minimize conflict in relationships and be in harmony with nature (Smith, 2009). This concept more simply stated would be to learn to "go with the flow". Attempting to exist in opposition to the Tao, one will eventually be consumed by it. Striving to live in harmony with the Tao or more specifically wu wei, will benefit from this relationship. Living more in harmony with the Tao can be often seen as being more out in the world and nature to experience its gifts while living a life interacting with nature as well as with others.

A second type of Taoism is "vitalizing" where practitioners strive to maximize their life force, also called *qi* or *chi*. These adepts worked with their minds, matter, and physical movement, to increase their life force (Smith, 2009). Some may find this branch of Taoism as more unusual or unfamiliar as Huston Smith called it a "vitality cult" (Smith, 2009). Most belief systems and/or religions are based upon the unknown, mysteries, and unconfirmed facts. To the uninformed, what is considered one person's religion may very well be another person's cult.

A third type of Taoism was influenced by Buddhism, being that of Religious Taoism. Here the actions of psychics, free-lance soothsayers, shamans, and faith healers who may have come by their powers naturally, religious Taoism institutionalized these activities (Smith, 2009). Religious Taoism appears as a crude superstition to the uneducated. At the time of Smith's observation, science knew little of what energy is, how it proceeds, or the means by which it can be utilized (Smith, 2009). However, currently, we do know about faith healing engaging energies, including faith in oneself. Placebos are now known and proven to have various healing effects mentally, physically, and/or spiritually.

I have had much firsthand experience with all 3 of these types of Taoism along with Buddhism and Confucianism, as a philosophical lifestyle, as my martial arts and qigong lineages are deeply rooted within these belief systems. I did not priorly nor formally study any of these philosophies but rather lived with them in my life. I see the concepts and principles found within these philosophies as being highly relevant to my everyday routine. I was raised within the Christian Church and more specifically the Lutheran and Disciples of Christ branches. Taoism does not oppose nor contradict these Christian faiths but rather supports morals and ethics found in many other religions.

The Taoist concept of *yin* and *yang*, where harmony and balance coexist, contrast and relativity are seen in all things in life and nature. Yin and yang ultimately affect all aspects of life in health, relationships, business, and even other religions in various other aspects. Yin and yang are much more than simply the contrast between dark and light. The symbol for this concept depicts cause and effect, ebb and flow, and other manifestations of harmony, and is known as the *Tajitu.* The symbol actually has more components than just the 2 fish-shaped halves. The complete circle itself consists of the two halves, plus the small dots of contrast found in each half, and lastly, the line that divides the two halves. These dots remind us that nothing is truly black or white, or absolute. The fine line resting between the two opposing halves may be viewed as the gray area that we sometimes find ourselves navigating when striving to balance our decisions. Decisions between what we perceive as true, right, or correct for whatever situation and circumstances relate to any particular time and place. What is seen as correct yesterday may not be so today; appropriate for one, may not be for another. These components collectively represent the ever-changing relationship of all of these various pieces and parts that make up the whole.

Meaning of the Yin-Yang Symbol

The yin and yang symbol or taijitu, relates to the day and night association of yin and yang. Supposedly the ancients plotted a graph made up of six concentrically larger rings. In the center was anchored an 8-foot high pole that measured the shadow cast by the sun throughout the seasons. Then they colored in where the shade landed and where there was none. When looked at from above, the graph showed a picture that resembles the yin and yang symbol but without the two dots on either side. From here the concept of balance and its relationship to the seasons and nature was conceived.

The yin-yang symbol has been long known to represent balance and harmony. However, some choose to label it as a religious symbol for Daoism which many consider more of a philosophy. The martial arts of tai chi uses this symbol and concept as a foundation to understanding of the flow of energy within the human body.

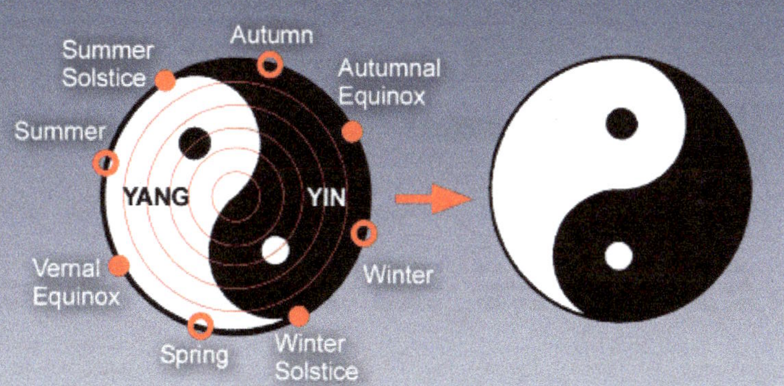

The Five Aspects of Yin and Yang

The 5 Aspects of yin and yang complement and balance each other via these aspects, which define the relationship between each.

1) Opposition

2) Interdependence

3) Mutual Consuming -Increasing

4) Mutual Transforming

5) Infinite Divisibility

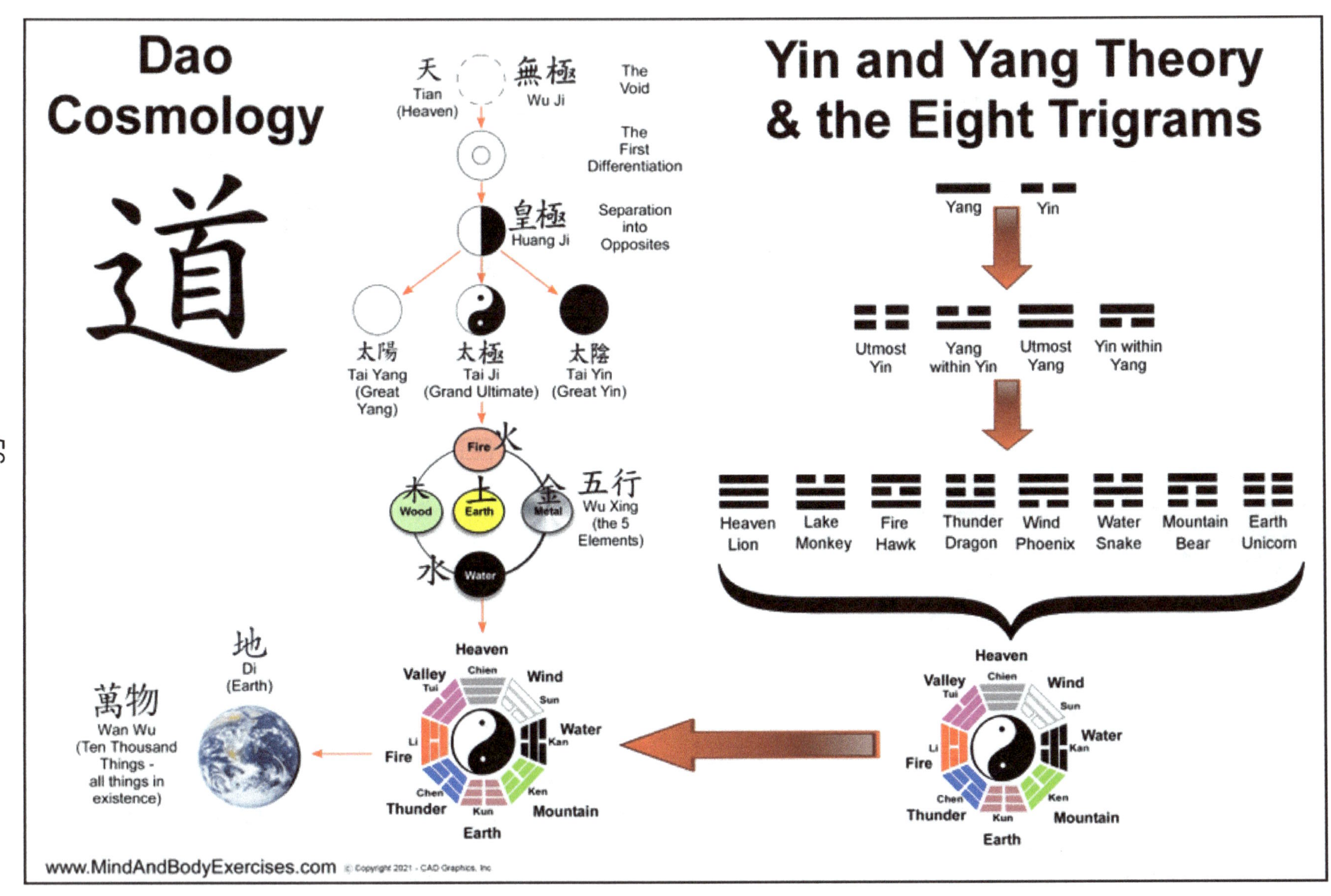

Dao
Cosmology
道
天
Tian
(Heaven)
無極
Wu Ji
The
Void
The
First
Differentiation
皇極
Huang Ji
Separation
into
Opposites
太陽
Tai Yang
(Great
Yang)
太極
Tai Ji
(Grand Ultimate)
太陰
Tai Yin
(Great Yin)
火
Fire
木
Wood
土
Earth
金
Metal
水
Water
五行
Wu Xing
(the 5
Elements)
Heaven
Chien
Valley
Tui
Wind
Sun
Water
Kan
Li
Fire
Chen
Thunder
Kun
Earth
Ken
Mountain
地
Di
(Earth)
萬物
Wan Wu
(Ten Thousand
Things -
all things in
existence)
Yin and Yang Theory
& the Eight Trigrams
Yang
Yin
Utmost
Yin
Yang
within Yin
Utmost
Yang
Yin within
Yang
Heaven
Lion
Lake
Monkey
Fire
Hawk
Thunder
Dragon
Wind
Phoenix
Water
Snake
Mountain
Bear
Earth
Unicom
Heaven
Chien
Valley
Tui
Wind
Sun
Water
Kan
Li
Fire
Chen
Thunder
Kun
Earth
Ken
Mountain
www.MindAndBodyExercises.com
© Copyright 2021 - CAD Graphics, Inc

Taoism does explain the creation of the Universe and what exists within it. The Tao transformed from the nothingness or *Wuji,* to yin and yang, then further into the 5 Elements or *Wuxing*, then to the 8 trigrams or *Bagua,* and eventually into the Ten Thousand Things. Some people may see these concepts as religious, while others may interpret as philosophy and maybe even others will see these ideas as a science of the universe.

The I Ching, a Taoist philosophical text written by Fu Xi around 1300 BCE, addresses 64 phases in that we go through in the process of becoming a human being (Hon, 2019). Through these phases, one can evolve from basically being unconscious to hopefully conscious, from an inferior to a superior human being. It actually takes considerable effort and time to become what we consider human. We are born basically like any other animal and more specifically a mammal, but with the potential abilities to learn to communicate and reason.

Upper trigram >> Lower trigram VV	Ch'ien	Chen	K'an	Kên	K'un	Sun	Li	Tui
Ch'ien	1	34	5	26	11	9	14	43
Chen	25	51	3	27	24	42	21	17
K'an	6	40	29	4	7	59	64	47
Kên	33	62	39	52	15	53	56	31
K'un	12	16	8	23	2	20	35	45
Sun	44	32	48	18	46	57	50	28
Li	13	55	63	22	36	37	30	49
Tui	10	54	60	41	19	61	38	58

Hexagrams of the I Ching

There is a fundamental belief within Taoism, that we are not born with the wisdom of being "correct" but rather we are born and begin to be "true" in our perceptions, words, and actions. For example, a child cries because they are hungry, expressing their true feelings of hunger pangs in their stomach. Later in life, that same child will learn that the correct way to express oneself may be to ask for food verbally.

We are usually not born as balanced or enlightened human beings. Humans are not intrinsically born as what we often label as "good". Our nature is seemingly good as an innocent little human being but basically, we are born as an animal with no inherent skill to survive physically or socially. Unguided children will not feed, clothe or potty-train themselves. If you look at any young child not nurtured, guided, or refined by a parent or mentor of that child, that child will instinctively do whatever they please until they meet with resistance. The child is not inherently "bad" but rather has instinctive behavior, similar to that of a little animal not knowing of boundaries or refinement. If the parent doesn't accept this duty of actual parenting, the child may eventually grow into an adult who spends their whole life behaving like an animal. If the parent does not take the time to give their child life direction by teaching with words and actions rooted in principle and love, that child will become a human being in physical form, while remaining an animal in their consciousness and relative actions.

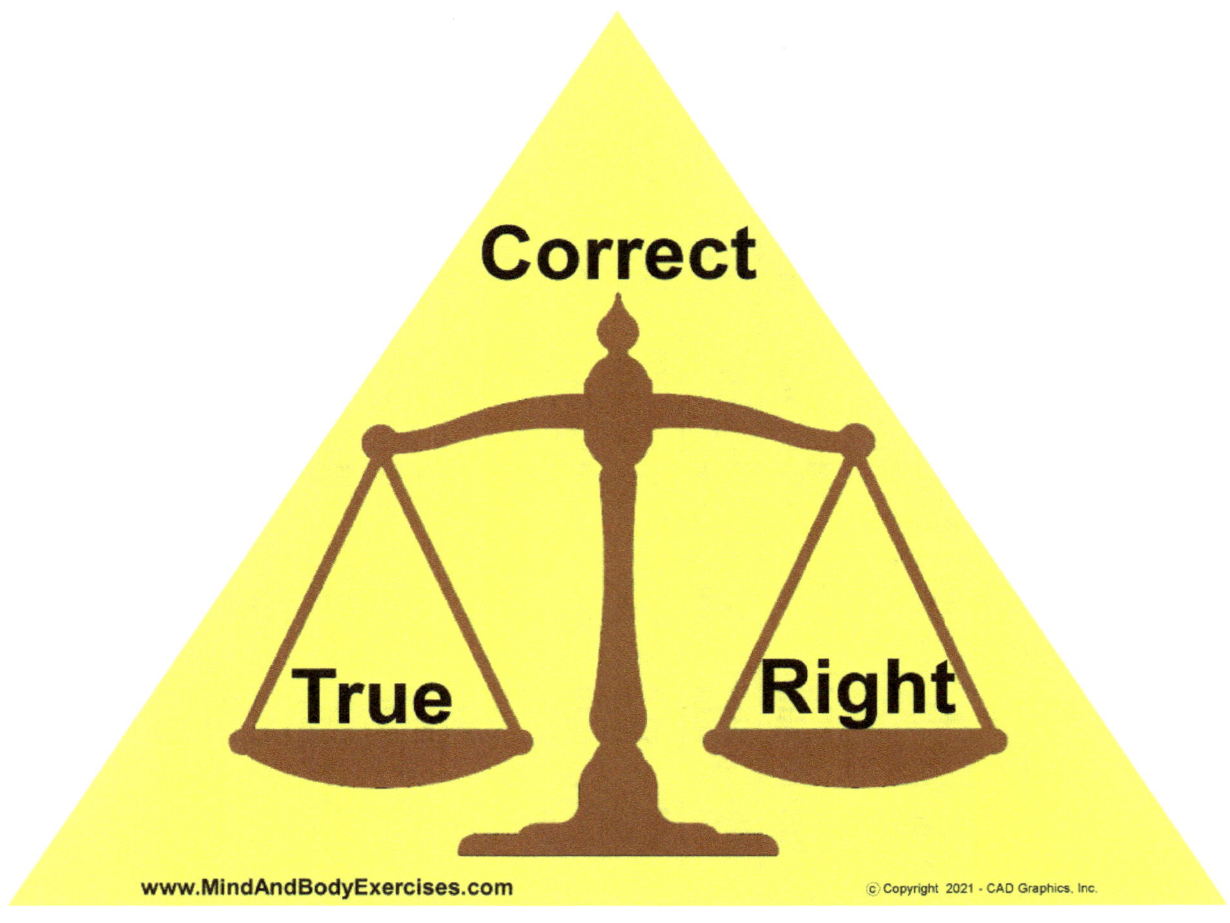

Some belief systems or philosophic schools of thought believe that we have to earn our human potential beyond that of being an animal. We are born into a particular set of circumstances or actions of cause and effect, known as *karma*, in Hinduism, Buddhism, and Taoism. Even before we arrive in the physical form of a zygote, embryo, or fetus, there is a belief structure that we already made an agreement based upon our karma, of what kind of resources one will come into this world with and relative life from these resources. These may include time and place of birth, physical or mental traits, ethnicity, status, and other cultural variables. Hopefully, the individual earned good karma in their past life because that affects where and to who they are born into.

Karma doesn't mean something that drops upon you from somewhere, Karma means your action, it's your making, it's your doing.

- Sadhguru

The first phase of life is childhood from birth to age 8, which is considered as Spring and is highly related to one's past karma. The individual child has very little control over their own current karma at this age, relying almost entirely upon where they were born and who their parents are. The order of the next phases of life would be Summer (ages 8-33), Late Summer (ages 33-58), Fall (ages 58-83), and Winter (ages 83-108). These phases of the year correspond accordingly with the 5 Element Theory or Wuxing (Wuxing, Internet Encyclopedia of Philosophy, n.d.), and the mental and physical changes we experience throughout our whole cycle of one lifetime.

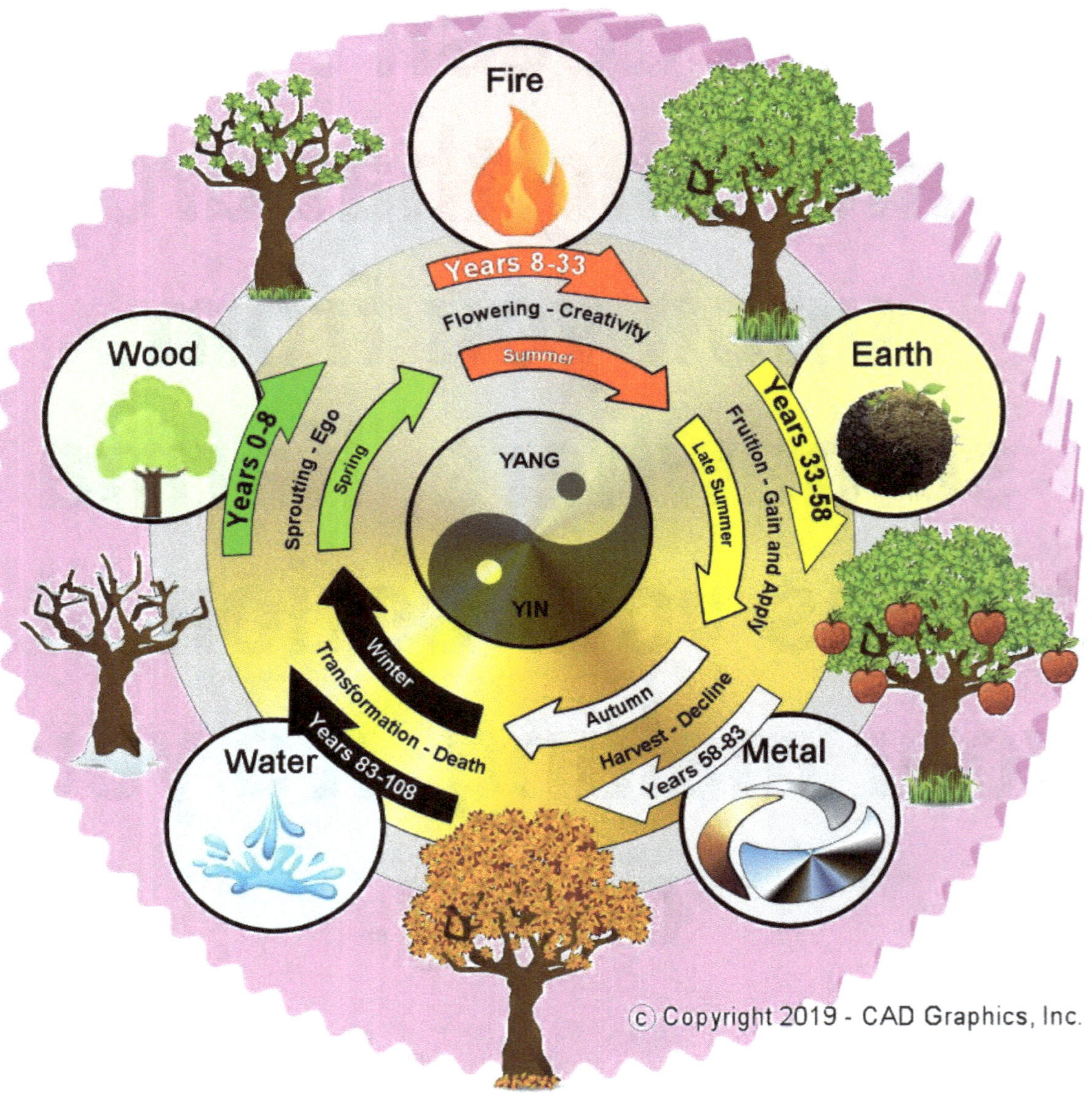

After the initial spring phase of childhood and into young adulthood or summer, the individual begins to work on choosing whether or not they are going to go through life in a state of unconscious suffering or go through life evolving as a conscious human being. Life is a challenge or struggle, and we all experience this struggle differently. The struggle never ends as we strive to become more human until we can no longer. Similar to standing upright on two feet, we always have a struggle to work and exert effort to stay standing. As soon as we stop working on standing, we fall. Consequently, there is this constant struggle to become more human or to use other labels such as self-realization or self-mastery. Realization in this context may be defined as having an advanced understanding of the interrelationship of their mind, body, and consciousness.

Self-cultivation is another appropriate term, as we ourselves are actually the garden that needs constant tending. Some among us may have started on this path decades long ago, trying to navigate within this lifestyle and path of self-cultivation. Some are considered spiritual teachers or leaders. They are not done yet, as we are never truly done as far as this physical life is concerned. If life is a constant struggle, the concept we have to accept is that no one is entitled to anything. If we truly want to change our reality, we need to realize that no one is going to change it for us. Not our friends, family, boss, government, or anyone other than ourselves. The universe and nature offer no entitlements that are going to change our individual reality. It starts with us taking ownership and responsibility to change our own set of circumstances and actions (karma) whether good or bad. If we look at our situations or circumstances as being someone else's fault or responsibility, we have lost control over our own life and our own potential outcomes. Ultimately, we may realize that we allow others the power to manage our lives until we choose to change this reality, as we alone choose to make ourselves good or make ourselves bad.

The concept of freewill

We have no true freedom if we are subject to the will of others. Self-cultivation is about taking total ownership of our own life and its direction. We have this choice every minute of every day, until death. Ancient and time-proven safe and effective methods of mind and body practices rooted in Buddhism and Taoism, such as yoga, tai chi, qigong, and other methods, offer ways to build character, strength, and self-discipline. Within some belief systems, these practices can affect one's karma. By regular and consistent execution in maintaining a particular posture or stance, despite the physical discomfort in doing so, the individual develops the fundamentals of self-discipline. These practices offer a very deliberate equation or recipe, to achieve self-cultivation. Self-cultivation cannot be achieved by luck or chance. Similar to traveling to a specific destination, one cannot easily reach their target by chance, without a map or sense of direction. Religions of Hinduism offer the *Yamas* and *Niyamas* whereas Christianity holds the 10 Commandments as guidance or maps of direction. Buddhism has the philosophy of the Eightfold Path and Islam has their 5 Pillars. The philosophy of Taoism has a similar guide in its own Eight-step Path.

This Eight-step Path of Taoism is where I will focus some attention. This path of processes is a map or recipe of insights that may lead to experiences in varying levels of evolution of our own consciousness. This recipe is rooted in the understanding that our life is basically a continuous yearly journey around the sun where we all go through the yearly cycles of the climatic seasons. The climate appears very random to us as children, where we see sun and rain for a while and then a time later of wind and snow. Until we are taught that there is a deliberate repeating cycle, this change in our surroundings, environment and relative weather patterns seems to be so random. When the child knowingly experiences a second or third year of the season changes, the climate becomes less confusing and actually more predictable. Similarly, the steps or cycles of the Eight-step Path may appear at first to be somewhat random but are quite deliberate.

The first step may be the most difficult, which is to truly see oneself in the highest expression of their humanness. The Sanskrit word of *namaste,* meaning of "may the divine in me see the divine in you". The challenge here is that in most cases, the individual cannot see the divine in others because they cannot see it first in themselves. This highly important component is in the reflection of actually looking inside of yourself. Often this step is most uncomfortable, where the individual is venturing outside of their comfort zone in order to go through the humility of seeing themselves in a less-than-perfect perspective. This is where methods of sitting, standing, and moving practices within yoga, qigong, tai chi, and others can offer these self-awareness reflections, in addition to their mere basic physical benefits of Westernized glorified stretching and breathing exercises. Beyond just exercising the body, these somewhat gentle methods can require the practitioner to become aware of their various aspects of weaknesses in their postural alignments, coordination, balance, and other facets of their self-awareness like breath and heart rate. Observing and becoming aware of our physical body is the gateway into becoming more aware of our complex thoughts and emotions.

The 8-Step Path to Achieve the Best Version of You

www.MindAndBodyExercises.com

A long-understood method of achieving harmony between one's mind, body and spirit, is this 8-Step Path. It has its origin in the ancient Chinese philosophy of Daoism but is highly relative to modern culture. The figure "8" is important to understand that as the infinity circle, there is no beginning nor end to entering into this process. It is a journey of self-awareness that can be entered into at any point throughout one's lifetime. Life is a challenge, and so is staying on this path of self-improvement. The reward is at the end of one's journey, knowing that they have pursued a meaningful life with direction and purpose.

1 Learning to Know Your "True Self"

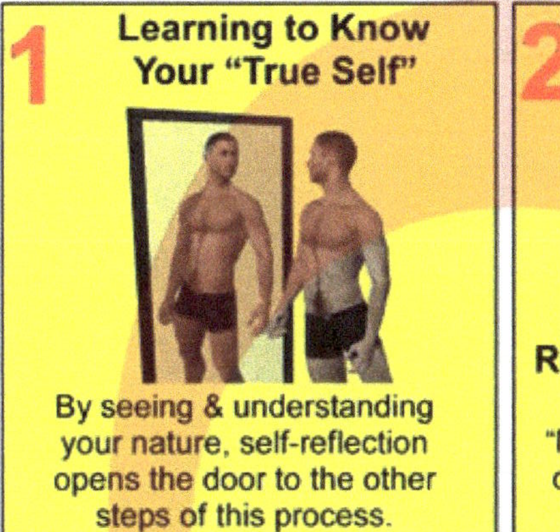

By seeing & understanding your nature, self-reflection opens the door to the other steps of this process.

2 Making Correct Daily Choices

True

Right ⟵ Correct

Awareness of an inner "Moral Compass" to balance decisions by understanding true, right & correct.

3 Overcome Delusion of Your Thoughts & Ideas

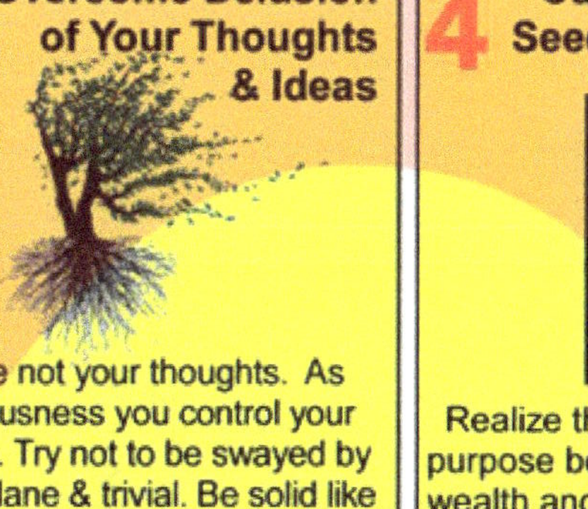

You are not your thoughts. As consciousness you control your thoughts. Try not to be swayed by the mundane & trivial. Be solid like the root & not flippant like the leaves.

4 Cultivate Good Seeds to Pass On

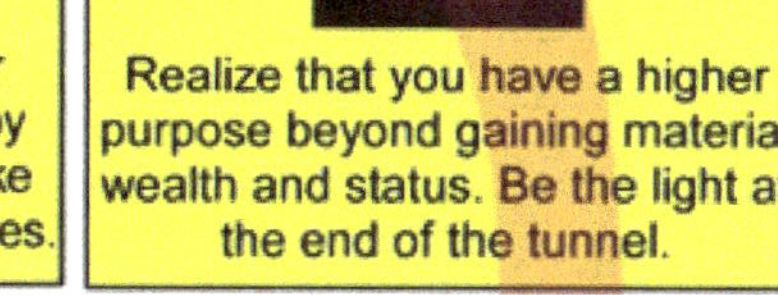

Realize that you have a higher purpose beyond gaining material wealth and status. Be the light at the end of the tunnel.

5 Attain Honor

Live by principle - stand firm in what you believe, while allowing challenges to flow around you. Stand like a mountain, flow like a river.

6 Change Your Reality

Understand that you are in control of your life and the choices you make determine your success or failure within your reality.

7 Become a Living Vessel of Wisdom

Knowledge alone is not power. The sharing of our knowledge, is when knowledge becomes powerful.

8 Draw on Nature's Power

Cultivate a strong mind, body & spirit by connecting to nature's fire, water & wind with sitting, standing & moving exercises.

We are not our thoughts, but rather the observer and master of them. Within the Tao Te Ching we find the wisdom text relating to reflection in (Novak, 1994):

> "Knowing others is intelligence,
> knowing yourself is true wisdom.
> Mastering others is strength,
> mastering yourself is true power.
> If you realize that you have enough,
> you are truly rich…"

We can seek to find the root causes of turbidity and chaos in our society today, where most people do not aspire to see their true selves and the chaos coming from within. This can be evident in our lack of taking ownership and accountability for any of our own behaviors. Self-reflection is a very important component of any belief system or spiritual cultivation. It is called reflection because in ancient times, mirrors did not exist. One would actually have to look at water in order to see their own image or a reflection thereof. If the water was moving or turbid it would not be possible to see one's reflection. Similarly, if one's thoughts and relative lifestyle are turbid, it is very difficult for one to self-reflect. Your mind is that water and so you never really get a chance to see your true nature because it's not very tranquil enough and never clear enough to reveal even just a fleeting glimpse of our true nature. This is an important component of spirituality, self-improvement, self-awareness, or whatever one chooses to call this concept. This nature of *our* higher nature isn't just *your* nature. It is *my* nature. It is *his and her* nature. It is *all of our* nature. It is all the same nature being that we are all basically connected. The divine in me sees the divine in all. We all have one little particle of that highest nature and when it is momentarily separated, we suffer the illusion of individuality for only a moment.

I do not see Taoism, Confucianism, or Buddhism as religions, but rather as life philosophies in that they hold principles that can easily be seen and/or incorporated into other spiritual belief systems. What I find most appealing about Taoism is that I don't find it to be a religion by definition, but rather a philosophy of how to navigate the human condition. I have found that Taoism at its core seeks to focus on holistic, universal, and peaceful principles of living in harmony with nature and the natural order of all within it, whether alive or inanimate.

Strive to see your true nature

References

Chinese Religions and Philosophies | National Geographic Society. (2022, May 20). National Geographic. Retrieved August 9, 2022, from https://education.nationalgeographic.org/resource/chinese-religions-and-philosophies/

Hon, Tze-Ki, "Chinese Philosophy of Change (Yijing)", The Stanford Encyclopedia of Philosophy (Summer 2019 Edition), Edward N. Zalta (ed.), URL = https://plato.stanford.edu/archives/sum2019/entries/chinese-change

Novak, P. (1994). The World's Wisdom. Retrieved from https://platform.virdocs.com/r/s/0/doc/122387/sp/178876424/mi/570541808?cfi=%2F4%5Btext%5D%2F2%5Bchapter06%5D%2F6%2F250%2F2%2C%2F1%3A0%2C%2F1%3A0

Smith, H. (2009). The World's Religions. Retrieved from https://platform.virdocs.com/r/s/0/doc/119147/sp/178692013/mi/570158024?cfi=%2F4%2F2%5Bch8%5D%2F4%2F182%2C%2F1%3A0%2C%2F1%3A0

Wuxing (Wu-hsing) | Internet Encyclopedia of Philosophy. (n.d.). Internet Encyclopedia of Philosophy. Retrieved August 9, 2022, from https://iep.utm.edu/wuxing/

Appendices

Glossary

Agency
The capacity to think, choose, and act independently. Agency reflects one's ability to direct behavior and make decisions based on personal values rather than external control.

Allostasis
The body's process of achieving stability through change. Rather than maintaining a fixed balance, the organism adapts dynamically to internal and external stressors.

Archetype
A universal pattern or symbolic model of behavior or identity. In this book, the Warrior, Scholar, and Sage function as archetypal expressions of human development.

Autonomic Nervous System (ANS)
A branch of the nervous system that regulates involuntary functions such as heart rate, digestion, and breathing. It includes the sympathetic (activation) and parasympathetic (restoration) systems.

Awareness
The ability to observe thoughts, emotions, and physical sensations without immediate reaction. Awareness is foundational to self-regulation and intentional behavior.

Bounded Choice
A condition in which individuals perceive themselves as free while operating within a restricted framework of options shaped by external influence or control.

Breath Regulation
The conscious control of breathing patterns to influence physiological and psychological states, including stress reduction and nervous system balance.

Cognitive Appraisal
The interpretation of a situation that determines emotional response. Different interpretations of the same event can produce different emotional outcomes.

Cognitive Flexibility
The ability to adapt thinking, shift perspectives, and revise beliefs when presented with new information or changing conditions.

Coherence
A state of alignment between thoughts, emotions, and physiological processes, often associated with improved performance and well-being.

Coniunctio
A term used in Jungian psychology referring to the integration or union of opposites within the psyche, leading to greater wholeness.

Consciousness
The state of being aware of one's internal and external environment. It includes perception, thought, and subjective experience.

Discernment
The ability to judge well, distinguish truth from distortion, and make decisions based on clarity rather than impulse or conditioning.

Emotional Regulation
The ability to manage and respond to emotional experiences in a controlled and adaptive manner.

Energetic Body
A conceptual model describing the body as an integrated system of dynamic processes, including breath, circulation, nervous system activity, and internal awareness.

Eustress
A positive form of stress that promotes growth, adaptation, and improved performance when applied appropriately.

Hermetic Principle
A foundational concept from Hermetic philosophy describing universal laws such as correspondence, polarity, and cause and effect.

Hormesis
A biological principle in which exposure to low levels of stress or challenge stimulates beneficial adaptive responses.

Identity Fusion
A psychological state in which an individual's identity becomes inseparable from a group, often reducing independent judgment and autonomy.

Ikigai
A Japanese concept referring to one's reason for being, combining purpose, passion, skill, and contribution.

Jing
In Traditional Chinese Medicine, the foundational essence of the body, associated with physical vitality, growth, and structural integrity.

Junzi
A Confucian concept describing an ideal person who embodies moral integrity, wisdom, and balanced character.

Locus of Control
The degree to which individuals believe they have control over the outcomes of their lives, either internally (self-directed) or externally (influenced by outside forces).

Meridian System
In Traditional Chinese Medicine, a network of pathways through which Qi is believed to circulate throughout the body.

Mindfulness
The practice of maintaining present-moment awareness with a non-reactive and non-judgmental attitude.

Neuroplasticity
The brain's ability to reorganize and form new neural connections in response to learning and experience.

Parasympathetic Nervous System
The branch of the autonomic nervous system responsible for rest, recovery, and restoration.

Polarity
The principle that opposing qualities exist on a continuum and can transform into one another depending on degree.

Psychological Flexibility
The capacity to adapt behavior and thinking in alignment with values, even in the presence of discomfort or uncertainty.

Qi (Chi)
In Traditional Chinese Medicine, the vital energy that animates and regulates physiological and psychological processes.

Resilience
The ability to recover from stress, adversity, or challenge while maintaining or returning to a functional state.

Self-Actualization
A concept from humanistic psychology describing the realization of one's full potential and capacities.

Self-Regulation
The ability to control thoughts, emotions, and behaviors in pursuit of long-term goals.

Shen
In Traditional Chinese Medicine, the aspect of consciousness or spirit associated with awareness, clarity, and emotional presence.

Somatic Awareness
The perception of internal bodily sensations, including posture, tension, breath, and movement.

Stress Response
The physiological and psychological reaction to perceived challenge or threat, involving activation of the nervous and endocrine systems.

Sympathetic Nervous System
The branch of the autonomic nervous system responsible for activation, alertness, and the fight-or-flight response.

Three Treasures (Jing–Qi–Shen)
A foundational concept in Traditional Chinese Medicine describing the integration of essence, energy, and consciousness.

Warrior
An archetypal aspect of development focused on action, discipline, physical training, and the capacity to confront challenge.

Scholar
An archetypal aspect focused on learning, inquiry, analysis, and the pursuit of understanding.

Sage
An archetypal aspect representing wisdom, integration, and the ability to apply knowledge with clarity and compassion.

Wu Wei
A Taoist concept meaning "effortless action," or acting in alignment with natural flow rather than force.

Yin and Yang
A foundational Taoist principle describing complementary opposites that exist in dynamic balance and constant transformation.

About the Instructor, Author & Artist - Jim Moltzan

While this book includes supplemental resources, its primary aim is not instruction, but integration supporting readers in understanding how healing unfolds across body, mind, meaning, and lived life.

My fitness training started at the age of 16 and has continued for almost 45 years. During that time, I attended high school, then college, and worked 2 jobs all while pursuing further training in martial arts and other fitness methods. Many years ago, I started up an additional business to help finance my next goal of owning my own school. I moved to Florida from the Midwest to make this goal a reality. Having owned two wellness and martial arts schools, I have surpassed what I once believed to be my potential. At this stage in my life, I have chosen not to open any more schools, as I found the business aspects took too much focus away from my true passion: training and teaching others.

Beyond my professional endeavors, I am also a husband and father of two grown children. I believe that we must be prepared to work hard mentally, physically and financially to earn our good health and well-being. Not only for ourselves but for our families as well. Good health always comes at a cost whether in time, effort, cost, sacrifice or some combination of the previous.

I returned to college in my later 50's, to pursue my BS in Holistic Health (wellness and alternative medicine). My degree program covered many wide-ranging topics such as anatomy and physiology, meditation, massage, nutrition, herbology, chemistry, biology, history and basis of various medical modalities such as allopathic, Traditional Chinese Medicine, Ayurveda/yoga, naturopathy, chiropractic, and complimentary alternative methods. I also studied religion, mythology of the world, stress relief/management as well as sociology, psychology (human behavior) and cultural issues associated with better health and wellness.

Most of the movements I teach and write about originate from Chinese martial arts. The Qigong (breathing work) is from Chinese Kung Fu and the Korean Dong Han medical Qigong lineage. I have also gained much knowledge of Traditional Chinese Medicine (TCM) from many TCM practitioners, martial arts masters, teachers and peers. This includes many techniques and practices of acupressure (reflexology, auricular, Jing Well, etc.), acupuncture, moxibustion as well as preparation of some herbal remedies and extracts for conditioning and injuries. I have been studying for over 20 years with Zen Wellness, learning medical Qigong as well as other Eastern methods of fitness, philosophy and self-cultivation. I have been recognized as a “Gold Coin” master instructor having trained and taught others for at least 10000 hours or roughly over 35 years. The core fitness movements are from Kung Fu and its forms in Tai Chi, Baguazhang, Dao Yin and Ship Pal Gi (Korean Kung Fu and weapons training). Each martial art has mental, physical and spiritual aspects that can complement and enhance one another. The more ways that you can move your body and engage your mind, the better it is for your overall health.

Physical health, mental well-being and the relationships within our lives; are these the most cherished aspects of our existence? Yet, how much effort do we put towards improving these areas on a daily basis? Many have used martial arts and other mind-body methods of training as methods of learning to see one's character as others see them. I feel that I can offer the priceless qualities of truth, honor and integrity with my instruction. You must seek the right teacher for you, because in time a student can become similar to their teacher. Through the training that I have experienced and offer to others, an individual can understand and hopefully reach their full potential.

By developing self-discipline to continuously execute and perfect sets of movements, an individual can start to understand not only how they work physically but also mentally and emotionally. You can find your strengths and your weaknesses and improve them both. Through disciplined training, one not only enhances physical abilities but also cultivates mental resilience, allowing them to achieve their fullest potential in all areas of life.

I have co-authored a book, produced numerous other books and journals, graphic charts and study guides related to the mind and body connection and how it relates to martial arts, fitness, and self-improvement. A few hundred of my classes and lectures are viewable on YouTube.com.

Lineage

- Recognized as a 1000 and 10,000-hour student and teacher
- Earned gold coins through the Doh Yi Masters and Zen Wellness program
- Earned a 5th degree in Korean Kung Fu through the Dong Han lineage

Education

Bachelor of Science in Holistic Medicine - Vermont State University

Books Available Through Amazon

https://www.amazon.com/author/jimmoltzan

Book Titles by Jim Moltzan

Book 1 - Alternative Exercises
Book 2 - Core Training
Book 3 - Strength Training
Book 4 - Combo of 1-3
Book 5 - Energizing Your Inner Strength
Book 6 - Methods to Achieve Better Wellness
Book 7 - Coaching & Instructor Training Guide
Book 8 - The 5 Elements & the Cycles of Change
Book 9 - Opening the 9 Gates & Filling 8 Vessels-Intro Set 1
Book 10 - Opening the 9 Gates & Filling 8 Vessels-sets 1 to 8
Book 11 - Meridians, Reflexology & Acupressure
Book 12 - Herbal Extracts, Dit Da Jow & Iron Palm Liniments
Book 13 - Deep Breathing Benefits for the Blood, Oxygen & Qi
Book 14 - Reflexology for Stroke Side Effects:
Book 15 - Iron Body & Iron Palm
Book 17 - Fascial Train Stretches & Chronic Pain Management
Book 18 - BaguaZhang
Book 19 - Tai Chi Fundamentals
Book 20 - Qigong (breath-work)
Book 21 - Wind & Water Make Fire
Book 22 - Back Pain Management
Book 23 - Journey Around the Sun-2nd Edition
Book 24 - Graphic Reference Book
Book 25 - Pulling Back the Curtain
Book 26 - Whole Health Wisdom: Navigating Holistic Wellness
Book 27 - The Wellness Chronicles (volume 1)
Book 28 - The Wellness Chronicles (volume 2)
Book 29 - The Wellness Chronicles (volume 3)
Book 30 - The Wellness Chronicles (complete edition, volumes 1-3)
Book 31 - Warrior, Scholar, Sage
Book 32 - The Wellness Chronicles (volume 4)
Book 33 - The Wellness Chronicles (volume 5)
Book 34 - Blindfolded Discipline
Book 35 - The Path of Integrity

Book 36 - Spiritual Enlightenment Across Traditions
Book 37 - Mudo Principles: Teachings from the Warrior, Scholar, and Sage
Book 38 – Hermeticism -Its Relevance to the Teachings of the Warrior, Scholar and Sage
Book 39 - Post Traumatic Growth
Book 40 - Post Traumatic Growth - Essays to Cultivate Healing, Integration, and Meaning
Book 41 - Architecture of the Human Journey – The Self-Healing Body
Book 42 - Architecture of the Human Journey – The Biological Mind
Book 43 - Architecture of the Human Journey – The Energetic Body
Book 44 - Architecture of the Human Journey – Embodied Discipline
Book 45 - Architecture of the Human Journey – The Healthcare Paradox
Book 46 - Architecture of the Human Journey – The Human Journey

https://www.amazon.com/author/jimmoltzan

Contacts

For more information regarding charts, products, classes and instruction:

www.MindAndBodyExercises.com
info@MindAndBodyExercises.com

www.youtube.com/c/MindandBodyExercises
www.MindAndBodyExercises.wordpress.com

407-234-0119

Social Media:

Facebook:	MindAndBodyExercises
Instagram:	MindAndBodyExercises
Twitter:	MindAndBodyExercise

Jim Moltzan - Mind and Body Exercises
522 Hunt Club Blvd. #305
Apopka, FL 32703

Website

Blog

YouTube Channel

www.ingramcontent.com/pod-product-compliance
Lightning Source LLC
LaVergne TN
LVHW081420110826
845149LV00010B/1814

9781958837603